CHARACTERS
IN PARADISE

A Yellowstone Memoir

Written by Fred Shellenberg

Edited by Linda Grosskopf

ISBN 10: 1-59152-070-3
ISBN 13: 978-1-59152-070-2

Cover: 1992 Mount Delano by Russell Chatham

You may order extra copies of this book by calling Farcountry Press toll free
at (800) 821-3874

Produced by Sweetgrass Books.

sweetgrassbooks
a division of Farcountry Press

PO Box 5630, Helena, MT 59604: (800)) 821-3874; www.sweetgrassbooks.com.

Printed in the United States of America

16 15 14 13 12 11 10   1 2 3 4 5 6 7

TABLE OF CONTENTS

INTRODUCTION

When I first laid eyes on it some forty years ago now, there was never a doubt in my mind why they named this singularly beautiful valley Paradise. And for sure there was no shortage of characters living in it, one good example being Don Nell from who I rented the old homestead I lived in up Deep Creek for twenty years. One of Don's best friends was Clayton Olson who had a automobile dealership in Livingston, and of whom Don, always with a straight face, would frequently remark, "he sells cars with no clutches." And there was Wilbur Lambert, who always helped me lay in firewood and who showed me what he knew of the fishing and hunting, which was plenty. One of his favorite isms was, "sex is the thing you can get the farthest behind on and catch up the quickest."

While Shellenberg's memoir does weave characters in and out of Park County, more importantly I think, it reviews his family history and limns his early life in other parts of Montana, his military duty during the second world war, and his stay on the frontier in Alaska. The vignettes are clearly all real, and they create an historical framework which brings the events to life. Perhaps this recollection's greatest strength is that it is told honestly and simply without a hint of artifice, in the voice of a proud, bona fide Native Son.

Russell Chatham

FOREWORD

This is not a book of fiction, and presumably, a book of facts needs a foreword or a prologue. You're not getting both, so here goes.

My foreword is primarily a disclaimer for those still living who may disagree with my version of the facts. When asked, the few acquaintances who have read this tell me that I have colored a few of the incidents incorrectly. Also, when four of my air crew had a small reunion in Livingston, I noticed that, when recounting experiences, there were always four slightly different versions… I lay this to their memories having failed somewhat, due to the aging process.

Actually, this was written for my kids and grandkids. It's life as I knew it and enjoyed it, and I hope that anyone reading it will get a few laughs along with the way things were in small town Livingston, Montana.

Fred Shellenberg
January 30, 2002

EDITOR'S NOTE

I met Fred Shellenberg at the wedding of his great-niece Corrine Estes and my nephew Clint Hammond in August of 2006. Fred made quite an impression on me as he brought with him to the wedding reception one of the books I have written for my autograph. I was, of course, delighted, and since that time, I have been pleased to sign a number of books not only for Fred but also for his nephew Jeff Shellenberg, who shares Fred's enthusiasm for collecting good Montana history.

Since 1985 with my first book, *On Flatwillow Creek: The Story of Montana's N Bar Ranch*, I have edited numerous people's material. These folks have, of course, had various educations and backgrounds, and their manuscripts have been in various conditions, ranging from scattered, handwritten notes to neat, well-organized data ready for final formatting. It's been a rare occasion when the material didn't require extensive reorganization to make it flow properly and easily from one paragraph to the next and from one chapter to the next. Fred's material has been a pleasure to work with because, with the exception of a few misspelled words and the need for some simple punctuation, the entire work was, almost without exception, "spot on" relative to organization, readability, and transitioning between paragraphs and chapters. Fred has the knack of telling his interesting material well and without the use of superfluous words. He's pretty much a "cut to the chase" man, and I found his material very easy to work with.

Like most authors, Fred was initially insulted when I said, with my usual amount of tact, that, while his material was great, it needed an editor to polish it up a bit and to re-format it in an eye-pleasing manner. With polite firmness, Fred declined my first offer to do that. However, not too many months later, he brought his manuscript to me once again. I had his number by then so, instead of getting the official okay to proceed, I got his material on my computer and edited, formatted, and sent him the beginning pages as well as the first three chapters presented in a nice three-ring notebook. About two minutes after the postman left the notebook in his hands, Fred sent me an email which read:

Dear Linda,

Wow! All systems go! Never argue with a freight train! It looks great.

Being almost human, I am never satisfied. I hope there will be a prominent "Linda Grosskopf" along with a foreword or a comment of some kind.

My thinking now is to try to get an appointment with a publisher and meet face to face. If your fertile brain comes up with either publisher or strategy, let me know.

As ever, Fred

So, freight train comment notwithstanding, it was been a pleasure and a privilege not only to get to know Fred better but also to be allowed to help him put his invaluable memories in publishable form.

Linda Grosskopf
January 24, 2010

Paradise Valley aligns the Yellowstone River south of Livingston, Montana. The spreading irrigated acres are seen here from Ponath Trail on the road to Luccock Park.

CHAPTER ONE

OLD TIMERS

One looks back and realizes it's not the work or even the play that one remembers most, but the people, the many people. History is presumably events that have transpired, but actually it's experiences of people that intermingle and overlap and cause these events to happen. And it is the distinct character and ambitions of people that make the different areas develop in different ways. Park County, Montana, has always been rich in people with distinct character and ambition.

I was at a relative's funeral the other day, and after a fine meal, my brother Art and I settled down on some porch chairs for a little visiting. A distant cousin came out and sat with us. I told her, "I was hoping a few of the old timers would show up today."

She informed me, *"You* are the old timers."

Where has the time gone? I can't ask neat guys that were about the age I am now to repeat those stories because they are all gone. History begins the day we are born. At first, we look forward to it, to what is going to happen. Then for quite a few years, we look ahead and back both, meeting all the people that tell us of bygone days and still working on our own aspirations. Then all of a sudden, the backward look encompasses more than the forward one.

All those great old guys, like D.A. and Howard Strong, that I remember from before going to school; and those great men from my adult years—like Bill Blome, Eb (Ebineezer) Strickland, Dan Miles, Johnny Hankins, the Harvats, and the great bunch that worked for Montana Power during the 1930s and '40s; and all those railroaders that worked in the shops and on the tracks and that ran those huge steam locomotives… These were Livingston and Park County people, and there were a lot of stories in all those characters and a lot of character in all their stories.

Why didn't I listen closer? My memory is poor, but I want to recount a few of the yarns they told that I still remember.

ELMER LEE

Elmer Lee was a character around town in the 1930s. He is the only man I ever knew that fought in the Spanish American War. Elmer was a big man, even rotund. He would chuckle deep down in his belly at his own stories. They were elaborate in detail and created suspense in any age listener.

With a little grandson on his knee, Elmer was yarning one time about a rich, lost gold mine, with emphatic hand gestures and a very confidential voice. When the story ended, the little boy looked up at his granddad with trusting innocent eyes and said, "Tell me another one, Grampa."

I'm going to try to tell another one or two.

BILL BLOME

Bill Blome moved here with his family in the late 1800s. His folks homesteaded on the head of Strickland Creek, which is on the Paradise Valley side of Wineglass Mountain. Bill tells of walking over the mountain when a boy with fresh vegetables to sell the miners at Chestnut. Chestnut was located about where the Trail Creek Exit is between Livingston and Bozeman. In his teens, Bill would haul wood to Livingston with team and wagon for the grand sum of $3 a load.

Bill went into the army during World War One at about age 30. After being discharged, he came back to the home place on Strickland Creek. He never spoke much of it, but he had some sort of disagreement with his father and brother. Eb Strickland told me it was over a few cows Bill had when he left for the service. After the disagreement, Bill walked off the place with a saddle over his shoulder and didn't go back for some 25 or 30 years.

When I knew Bill, he had nothing but good to say about his brother Ed, who still lived on the old place. "He's the best rancher in the valley," Bill would say. "He doesn't have all that expensive plowing and farming machinery; he just puts up hay and runs cows."

When Bill and his brother Ed finally ran into each other at

an auction sale, they could hardly let go of each other when they shook hands. They had great times after that visiting and wondering why they had been so stubborn all those years... It's a sad commentary on human nature that we do not get along with those we should, but it happened long ago, and it still happens.

They weren't the only ones that were stubborn. Those homesteading days were hard time for most of the settlers. In some circumstances, it made for having trouble with neighbors.

DEVIL'S LANES

Bill explained "Devil's Lanes" to me. When two adjoining homesteaders weren't getting along too well, one of them would build his fence line a few feet inside the surveyed line and then would not let his neighbor tie onto the corner which was on his property. That would force the neighbor to build another fence with his own corner, creating a lane between the two fences.

The law stated that access had to be given to land that didn't face a road. Then there would be two gates to open at the double fence line. A refinement in this feud was when you closed your own gate and left the neighbor's gate open. Then his cows would get into these lanes between the fences; hence the term "Devil's Lanes." Some of these lanes happened on Strickland Creek and also up Mission Creek.

ANDY DALY

After World War One, Bill worked as a ranch hand until the next World War. Then, as he stated, he got a "real job" laying brick on the new shop addition the Northern Pacific was building in Livingston. Bill never married, and most of the ranch years were spent working for Andy Daly, above Daly Lake and in the Daly Basin. I never met Andy Daly but heard many good stories about him.

Andy told Bill one day, "When I came out here, the Daly family settled in the Gallatin Valley for one year. We had our choice of practically the whole valley. Have you ever wondered why I settled on this rock pile?"

"As a matter of fact, I have," said Bill. "The Gallatin was a rich valley, but I could see there would be plowing to do and lots of machinery to buy. I just wanted to put up a little hay and hang onto a cow's tail. I could buy most of those valley men today."

Bill tells of a time when he and Andy were just finishing haying for the year. Andy had made the last sweep with the buck rake, and the stack was topped off. Andy headed across the field toward the barn. About half way across, he stopped the team, got off the buck rake, took out his pocket knife, and cut off some grass that the mower had missed on a corner. Something spooked the team, or maybe they were just anxious to get home. In any case, they ran away, the buck rake was wrecked, and the team got into wire. After the mess was cleaned up, Bill asked, "Andy, was it really worthwhile to cut those few blades of grass?"

Andy said, "I like a clean field."

Andy was a hard-riding cowboy, and Bill told many stories of handling cattle and horses in that rock-filled corral at the Daly Ranch. However, there came a day when Andy felt he was a little too old for breaking horses. He had one to break and approached Wesley D'Ewart to break it for him. This is when Wes D'Ewart first came to the country. He was a forest ranger for the Gardiner district and came from Back East—before Wes ranched up Wilsall way and before he became a United States Representative.

Bill always ate in the ranch house with Andy and Agnes Daly. One morning during breakfast, Wes brought the horse back. Wes had a sort of Back East accent and didn't pronounce his Rs completely. He told Andy, "He is well broke, but you can't use spuhs on him."

Andy's only reaction was, "Aggie, get my spurs."

Those old timers had to figure things out for themselves.

The corral just up the little creek from the Daly ranch house was still in use in the '50s when I first started hunting up Daly Basin. It was half rocks, some as big as wheelbarrows. Bill tells of trying to corral a bull. After several attempts, Andy rode alongside the bull, roped him, and on a dead run, turned him and dragged him into the corral without breaking stride. "Now you can shut the gate," said Andy.

I didn't know Bill until in the '50s when I was milking cows and custom baling hay. Bill had retired to a very small place where he could keep a couple cows or a few yearlings. "I've hung onto a cow's tail all my life, and it's too late to let go now." Bill helped his neighbors with haying or other chores. Many of the neighbors and their kids would visit the Blome house, and the coffee pot was always on and there was something good for the kids.

After a hard week of pitching bales, my brother and I went over to Bill's one evening for a little rest and a visit. On entering the house, we found Bill seated at the table with a big bottle of liniment. He'd pour some into one hand and rub it on this shoulder, take a couple of swigs, and then pour some into the other hand for the other shoulder. "Good for man or beast, internally or externally," said Bill.

When work wasn't too pressing, several of us had a little ritual of taking in the weekly auction at Bozeman Livestock Commission Co. It was a pleasant break, sometimes buying a bargain or just checking the market. Invariably on the way home when coming over the top of the Bozeman Hill, Bill would say, "I tell you, boys, it's sure good to get back into Park County."

EB STRICKLAND

Sometime in the late '20s or early '30s, Bill and Eb Strickland were partners on the Strickland Ranch on Strickland Creek. This place is now part of Allyn O'Hair's holdings. Bill and Eb were lifelong friends, and they knew the same people. The difference was Bill remembered all the dates and stories. Eb would grumble, "Who would want to remember all that stuff?" Eb was more interested in current frustrations and would make statements like, "How can those kids of mine borrow my car, then put it back in the garage, and there isn't enough gas left in it to back it out?"

In later years, I found out that the boys would drain the gas out of it. Eb would get backed into the alley and run out of gas. This was just a good joke on their dad.

When Eb was complaining about the doings of his boys, Bill would remind him, "Mothers used to take their kids off the streets when you rode your horse into town some 50 years ago."

Bill claimed Eb was the first white child born in Park County. I never heard Eb express an opinion one way or the other. Neither of them would remember the birth, and I'm sure there are several claims to that distinction. Eb was married to Andy Daly's adopted daughter, but as Bill always said, Eb was more of a Daly than his wife was. Eb's mother was a sister to the Daly brothers that settled here.

Eb always enjoyed being where the action was, but normally didn't contribute much more than advice. One time, however, we were branding some odds and ends purchased at the Bozeman yards. There was a little 400-pound black heifer in the load that was kind of crazy, one of those that hold its head up kind of high and funny. That little thing could put a grown man on the fence!

I was working the squeeze chute and missed that heifer coming out. Why Eb was standing outside with a rope I don't know, but he dabbed a loop on the calf, and then that 80-year-old man set his heels and threw that heifer when she hit the end of the rope. My brother and I jumped on it to hold it down, but it struggled up. We managed to grab the rope, and that little critter drug us for a hundred yards before we finally choked it down enough to get on it again and administer the brand and vaccination.

Eb Strickland gave me the only firsthand account of the early livestock business. The Daly family was running cattle in the upper Paradise Valley even before the railroad came through Park County. There were no fences or corrals. Very little hay was produced. If left to themselves, the cattle would inhabit the river bottoms the year around. They also preferred the bottoms to get some alkaline as salting cattle was not yet a common practice in the livestock industry. This alone caused them to migrate to lower areas.

Consequently, most of the summer was spent keeping the cattle at higher elevations to preserve feed in the bottoms for winter use. Some of the horses were always kept in the barn and fed. Eb and Bill both claimed that, in severe weather or when snow was crusted and made it difficult for cattle to forage, they would haul out loads of horse manure for the cattle. The partly digested feed that went through a horse made the first supplemental feeding. Bill referred to it as "just like feeding cubes."

Eb said, in the fall when the cattle came out of the high country, the Daly brothers would hold a roundup and put their own separate brands on the calves. The cattle were held between the river and the bluffs near Wannigan. Eb recalled one brother quirting another while arguing over a calf, and, Eb added, the calf wasn't worth anything as there was really no way to market them.

An interesting sidelight to the branding is that Andy Daly's brand, one of the first, was "Q". Andy Strickland, Eb's oldest son, still had the Q brand registered when he died a few years ago.

CHAPTER TWO

HOW IT WAS

In seventy some odd years, there is considerable change, but on the other hand, very little change. We, of course, begin our thinking of happenings before our own time. Olin D. Wheeler wrote a substantive history, "The Trail of Lewis and Clark," published in 1904 to coincide with the 100th anniversary of the expedition. There is a photograph entitled the Gates of the Mountains, which is looking from the west side of Livingston through the canyon toward the Paradise Valley. There is one rail of a railroad track in the very bottom of the photo. It is where the rail turns west beyond the 7th Street Y. There are two telegraph poles along the track and two fences showing, one of them the right of way fence for the rails. There is no discernable road or structure or any trees, even along the creek, in the open three-mile stretch of land from Livingston to the mouth of the canyon. Obviously, the photo was taken prior to 1904, the publication year of the book, but certainly after the railroad arrived in Livingston in 1882. The rail was not completed to the coast until 1883 when the golden spike was driven on September 8. The branch line to Gardiner was started prior to the golden spike ceremony. Could this photograph have been taken by the Northern Pacific railroad photographer, F. Jay Haynes, between this short span of time 1882 to 1883 when the Yellowstone branch line was started? At any rate, there has been considerable change in that wide open area south of Livingston to the canyon, with not only the remnants of the railroad branch line to Gardiner, but with a highway, an exit off the interstate, many mature trees, and countless structures, irrigation canals, and power lines. My life until after high school was spent in that area between town and the canyon, where things are still changing with supermarkets, motels, and auto dealerships. We may have to look back further than one lifetime for real change, but not for minor changes.

Transportation & Utilities

My first recollections, of course, included the automobile and most of the buildings that are still on Main Street. However, when I attended middle school in the 1930s, the large parking lot on B Street across from the fly fishing center nearly always had teams of horses with a wagon and a few saddlehorses tied to some billboard signs. There were still a few houses in the city and most outside of town that did not have a sewer or septic system. Most of the country places didn't have electricity with both town and country cooling food with ice boxes, utilizing blocks of ice. Livingston's ice was sawed from a pond on the end of 9th Street across from the old waterworks. There was a large storage building there, in which the ice would be covered with sawdust and kept until the next winter when a new freeze started. We kids would get chips of ice to suck on when the iceman was chipping off chunks for house delivery.

GREAT DEPRESSION

These are conveniences that are still improving, from engines to jets and from the industrial age to the computer age. But probably the greatest concern in the 1920s and 1930s was the Great Depression. I feel Livingston never really felt the brunt of this. I don't believe anyone actually went hungry. Many people had gardens and canned much food. They ate wild meat, and many homemakers sewed their own and their kids' clothes. Livingston still had a town herd of milk cows, which I'm sure provided for family and relatives. During summer, these cows were herded by some enterprising kid in the Green Acres area. I don't know who owned the land, but they apparently didn't care if someone herded 15 or 20 cows on it. The herder would come back across the tracks on the east end. As he came west on Callander Street, each cow would drop off and go down the alley to its own barn. Many people had chickens for both meat and eggs, and chicken feed sacks were used as material for sewing.

Livingston had automobile dealerships, clothing stores, shoe stores, many grocery stores, hardware stores, and lumber yards. Nearly everything anyone could want was available on Main Street. Now people think nothing of driving to Bozeman or Billings just to shop for a pair of shoes.

THE GOVERNMENT

The government entered the communities and lives of people more in the 1930s with programs to promote employment and improve infrastructure. The CCC (Civilian Conservation Corps) built many trails in the national forest, and there is still much of the road and trail complex in Yellowstone Park being used. The WPA (Works Progress Administration) built schools and various other structures in towns and cities. Livingston had a large remodeling and addition to their high school, then located on 5th Street. Other projects were the Civic Center and the Yellowstone Street bridge to Sacajawea Park.

CHAPTER THREE

THE STAFF OF LIFE

As with many people of my generation and in my case in early married life, wild game was considered a staple. Deer meat was cheaper than eating a young beef that could be sold for $75 or $100. Very few hunters were looking for trophies, although a large rack of horns was kind of a bonus. Very few hunters mounted trophy heads. Most of the ambitious ones nailed the horns to the woodshed, and a few of us just threw them up on the roof of the shed with the firm intention of nailing them up as time allowed.

Most of the game taken and consumed was fully legal. However occasionally, due to extenuating circumstances and or circumstances beyond one's control, an extra animal was taken during season and, very rarely, out of season.

MISUNDERSTANDING

I recall one such incident when Wes Strong, my brother-in-law, was putting up hay on the Cobb place on Suce Creek. His uncle Howard Strong was viewing the operation when a four-point buck walked into the field. His horns were in the velvet, and Howard jokingly said, "I sure would like a set of those for my collection."

The next day, Wes drove into Howard's place along the river, pulled a set of velvet horns out of the Jeep, and handed them to his uncle. "Here are those horns you wanted."

Howard almost had a fit. "You dang fool, what's the matter with you?"

There was an old dry well on the place that had wooden cribbing extending two or three feet out of the top of it. It was only about 10 feet deep and never had water in it except during high water on the river. Nothing could fall into it too easily but it should have been filled. Howard grabbed the horns, threw them into the well, and started shoveling dirt on top of them. The horns were wasted, but the meat wasn't, and that old well was filled. This wasn't really poaching. It was just that one joke can lead to another.

MAD MAMA

One instance of true poaching, however, was when my brother and Wilfred Thomason were haying some mountain meadows and felt the need of fresh meat. On the way out that evening, they shot a deer and hung it in the garage at my mother's place. It was warm so they skinned it right away and cut up the meat. My mom was a nervous wreck. The meat was packed and in the freezer, but that fresh hide was laying around. The next morning she fired up the wood stove in the kitchen, cut that fresh deer skin into strips, and burned it. It took her all day and the smell of burning hair was rampant. She informed the culprits, "Don't you knuckleheads ever bring anything like that to my place again."

WILFRED THOMASON

Wilfred Thomason was a brother to Bernice Fuhrer, the lady that introduced me to my wife. He had also been raised in the Gibson country my mother came from. He was a hunting fool. He hunted rocks, big game, small game, rattlesnakes, or anything that gave him an excuse to be on the river or in the hills. Big game outfitters were rare in the '30s. Wilfred was my earliest acquaintance with an outfitter; perhaps the term "hunting guide" would be more appropriate, as he did not really outfit anyone.

In the 1930s, elk did not inhabit all of the mountain ranges as they do now. Harsh winters would force many Yellowstone Park elk to migrate out in search of feed. Between Gardiner and Jardine, hundreds and even thousands of elk would cross the Yellowstone River, migrating into the lower areas with Jardine being sort of an epicenter of hunting activity. This was known as the firing line, and some mornings there were hundreds of hunters, with gunfire starting at sunrise. It would sound like a battle skirmish, and a few men were accidently killed, as bullets and ricochets were going in all directions.

Wilfred would take two or three hunters to the firing line; he charged them $5 each and guaranteed them an elk. Wil told me how the operation worked. They would get up on the line, and he would drop an elk for each of his clients. I told Wil he wouldn't get $5 from me unless I shot my own.

"Those guys think they dropped one themselves. I would be off to the side and I'd tell them, 'Nice shot, Jim,' or, 'You sure nailed him, Joe.'" Most of those guys couldn't hit a thing, but Wilfred filled their tags with sensitivity and feeling, giving them the bragging rights free.

You Can Always Tell A Poacher

Don Wood, who has boarded a few hundred deer for years on his ranch near Springdale, says you can always tell a poacher because he never gets any blood on himself when dressing an animal. Don says he knows one banker that hunts in a business suit and never gets it dirty. This definition certainly absolves me and most of the people I hunt with of poaching. When I finish dressing out an animal, everybody knows it as I'm blood from head to foot.

During high school and my young adult years, it was customary, and still occasionally indulged in, to drag Main and Second Street with a deer or elk draped over the front fenders or the back of a pickup. It was just an unassuming and gentle way of telling the world, "Look what a great hunter I am."

ACCIDENTS HAPPEN

Opportunity sometimes presents itself in too many easy shots. I recall two friends of mine hunting elk in Daly Basin. Five of these easy shots walked through a clearing. Bill and Low dropped the last two in line without spooking the other three. Somebody said, "There are plenty of empty tags in Livingston," and three more elk bit the dust. They were way back in the basin, and after dressing them out, it was nearly dark, and they headed for Livingston. I had one of the first Jeeps that wasn't military, a 1946 or '47, I think, so I was one of the empty tags. The snow was about a foot deep and partly blown off the ridges. However the elk were in such rough terrain that a jeep could not drag them all the way. We enlisted one of Henry D'Ewart's kids, about 14 years old, and his horse to help with the tough skidding.

Finally after much brute work and the help of the horse, we had five elk assembled where the jeep was parked. We hooked on to them in tandem and headed out. It was nearly all downhill, but our real problem rose when we came to a side hill. Those five elk were strung out a long ways and started sliding down the hill. The back of the jeep was sliding too. The bottom of the draw was full of brush and deep snow. It would take a week to get everything out if we slid in there. The rope knots were frozen, and Bill was running along, trying to cut a one-inch frozen rope with a dull knife. Fortunately, he didn't get the job done before we finally got around the hill to flatter ground and those elk behaved and strung out straight behind us again.

On the way up, we left a flat bed hay trailer at the Daly ranch house. We got there with the elk about eight o'clock and loaded them on the trailer. It was about 10 below zero, and that jeep didn't have doors. It was dark, cold, and miserable and from Daly's Lake to the Wanigan seemed like 100 miles. Fortunately, the Wanigan was still open or the Whithorns would have been rousted out of bed. We had a cup of coffee and partly thawed out and then went on to Livingston. Looking back on a trip like that makes one realize how much younger, dumber, and hungrier we must have been than we are now.

Another time, Bill Strong and I were hunting elk on the head of Davis Creek, just over the divide from the south fork of Deep Creek. We had packed in from the West Boulder side and had a camp a mile or so below where the trail goes over the top to Deep Creek.

The next morning we headed up the creek and within an hour spotted a bunch of 15 or 20 elk. They were drifting into the timber and would probably bed down. We discussed our strategy and split up, planning to approach them from two sides. The approach was perfect, and we both connected. The problem arose when Bill didn't hear my shot and connected twice. So purely accidentally, we had three good elk.

About the time we had everything dressed out, an airplane few over. The elk were pretty much in the timber, but the plane circled and looked us over. Bill, who tends to be a worrier, knew it was the game warden. I tried to reassure him and myself that the elk should be hard to spot, being partly in the timber.

We headed for camp and the horses. We fed and watered the pack horse, leaving him in camp, climbed on the other two, and hightailed it out, going over the divide and out Deep Creek as it was the shorter way home. Our first stop was the Allen Nelson ranch. Allen then lived just below the Deep Creek ranger station. Allen had an unused tag so that part was taken care of. He couldn't or wouldn't go back with us the next day, however, but offered Jack Munro's services. Jack was working for Allen at the time and was a good man with horses and packing.

We left the horses at Nelsons, planning an early start, and hitched a ride to town. While Bill was eating supper, one of his kids answered the phone and said, "Dad, the game warden wants to talk to you."

Bill blanched and could hardly stammer out, "H-h-hello, J-j-joe."

Joe Gaab inquired as to the success of the hunt and when we planned to go back in to bring out the game. Bill's answer was, "Tomorrow morning."

"How early are you leaving? I'll ride in with you."

"P-p-pretty early, Joe."

"How early?"

"About f-f-five."

"That's a little early. I'll meet you up there."

"Ok-k-kay, J-j-joe."

Bill was in a panic and immediately drove over to my house, where the panic was contagious. "We'll just have to explain it to him."

"Yeah, but you'll lose your rifle."

"I'm not lying to the sucker" and back and forth and back and forth.

My wife made the observation, "If I ever take up a life of crime, I'll not take you two with me."

We finally decided I would pick Bill up at 3:30 a.m., and we'd have breakfast at my house. We let Jack know departure would be between 4 and 4:30 am. The die was cast. I couldn't sleep worth a hoot and went to pick up Bill before 3:30. The house was all lit up, and he had his wife Mary sewing sheets for game bags. We had never used game bags before; nor have we since. But when Bill can't sleep, nobody sleeps. He couldn't agonize alone so he had his poor wife up to help him. I don't remember even taking the game bags with us.

Vi had a great breakfast ready—bacon, eggs, and pancakes. I don't think we ate three bites between us. It's the only time I can remember not being hungry. We drove by Joe Gaab's house; it was still dark, which gave us a little respite. Jack had the horses ready, and by 4:30, we were heading up the mountain. We had to use flashlights to find the trail in one place. We pushed as fast as possible, got over the top, down the Davis Creek side, and had our elk tagged just about daybreak.

We were just relaxing for the first time in about 24 hours when Joe Gaab came down the switchbacks, leading an empty pack-horse. He had left 2 hours after we did and got there just shortly after we did. That man had good horses and knew how to use them. Joe checked the tags, and everything was fine except I had punched the wrong date, which brought out, "You dumb sucker" from Bill. Joe let me punch the right date and graciously took half an elk on his empty horse and left us, heading down Davis Creek. We picked up our other horse and camp, put a half an elk on each horse, and lead our string out, completing two days' work in one day, thanks to Joe's help.

No Disguising Venison

These little incidents might lead one to believe we lived our lives at the edge of the law. This is not the case, but the exception. There was not quite the stigma many people now have about hunting in this manner, this being long before the animal rights' people were making the impassioned plea that it's a sin against nature to shoot a buffalo and that they should be saved for wolves to eat them alive.

A wild game diet certainly helps with the grocery bill, but somehow or other most people tire of it more so than beef or ham. The next step is to disguise the meat in various ways. Making sausage and jerky is popular. Once I cured two quarters with salt brine and smoking, similar to making ham or bacon. The first meal was good and tasted just like ham, but the next time, it again tasted like deer.

During some early lean years, my sister religiously prepared deer steak nearly every day, made gravy with the drippings, and fed most the meat to the dog.

Just before Thanksgiving a few years ago, Vi and I met Tom Osen and his wife in the grocery store. A few pleasantries were exchanged, and I commented about doing Thanksgiving shopping. Tom said, "We're having whitefish for Thanksgiving, but with the price of maggots, we can hardly afford whitefish anymore." Now there is a man that can carry an exaggeration into new and unexplored heights, but implies an old mindset. I'm sure many people have graced their table with wild game even for holidays.

Hunting and fishing are grand and practical sports. Most Montanans have engaged in them. My kids now hunt and enjoy the meat. Very little game goes to waste, and it fulfills one's desire to live at least partially off the land.

CHAPTER FOUR

COWBOYING, FARMER STYLE

D r. Loren Evans, now of Ronan, Montana, is one of my brothers-in-law. He retired from the University of Pennsylvania as a veterinarian and head of surgery of the world famous horse clinic at Kennet Square. He has worked on nearly all of the famous horses of the past 30 years. He has had consultations and held seminars from Ireland to South Africa and South America. I think it is an understatement to call him an authority on horses.

EXPERTS DON'T ALWAYS KNOW EVERYTHING

However, some years ago at an Evans' reunion in Polson, a friend invited Loren along to salt some cattle. Loren accepted, and I tagged along. The friend pulled into the yard with a saddled horse on a flatbed, stake-body pickup. The panels on the pickup bed came to just higher than the horse's knees. We piled in and drove about 10 miles south of town. We turned into a pasture and stopped at a swampy creek. That's where the horse came in. Loren's friend tied a couple blocks of salt to the saddle, climbed on, crossed the creek, and dropped the salt over a fence on the other side. The pickup was parked on flat ground. To unload the horse, a rear panel had been taken out, and the animal jumped to the ground. When this cowboy came back, the horse jumped into the bed of the pickup and was retied; the panel was put back. That horse jumped in and out like a dog would, and Loren stood there in open-mouth astonishment. "How do you teach a horse to do that?"

"Loren, I have tried to tell you that animals are *not* pets. They were put here to do some work, and you just have to let them know what you want done."

Now that's what I call the epitome of horsemanship. I have been around horses at various times most of my life. I like horses and consider them a very aesthetic animal. However, when there is a disagreement on how something should be done, the horse generally wins out. The horse never seems to understand exactly what I had in mind.

PLAN B

One year, Bill Strong and I were going elk hunting. We were leaving in the late afternoon. Actually, I couldn't leave until after five, so Bill saddled and packed and took off up the trail before I got there. My horse was tied to a tree at the trail head, and I took off just about dusk. About a mile up the trail, there was some down timber. That horse would not step across it. I tried running him at it to make him jump, and I tried leading him across it. I picked up a front leg and put it over the log, but no go. I finally jerked the saddle and bridle off him and left him standing there, shouldered my rifle, and walked four or five miles into the camp my partner had all set up.

TULE

I once purchased a nice little bay mare from Austin Swandal. She was ten years old and well broke. Austin was a real horseman; hence, his horses knew their manners. Austin must have hauled her into Livingston for me as I don't remember loading her at Wilsall. About a week later, I was going to load her on a trailer and go somewhere. Most homemade trailers of that time dropped the end gate, which formed a ramp for the animal to walk on. I walked up into the trailer leading Tule at a brisk walk. About half way in, I nearly fell backwards with the lead rope going in the wrong direction. That gentle little mare was hunkered back like a stubborn mule. I tried everything. I even picked up each front foot and placed them on the ramp and then went to the other end and pushed. I then resorted to the final try of winching her in by putting the rope through the ring in front of the trailer and keeping the slack out. This is an ideal way to bust up the trailer or break the halter. I just started looping the rope into the ring when Tule nearly knocked me down getting into the outfit. On looking up, I saw an old guy walking by with an irrigating shovel over his shoulder. Tule thought she was going to get a whack across the rear and was avoiding it. As a matter of continuing history, she never again gave me trouble loading. She apparently thought I could conjure up a guy with a shovel any time it was needed.

How NOT To Lead A Horse

Most horses are gentle by nature, but the gentlest animal can get upset if things go haywire. Once, my brother was helping Wes and Dennis Strong move some cattle. It was raining, it was cold, and the cattle were strung out on a county road heading for summer pasture. Art figured it would be warmer walking so he tied the reins, looped them over his wrist, and put his hands in his slicker pockets. Art aimed a little kick at a slow calf, the slicker flapped, and the horse took off. Art couldn't get his hands out of his pockets, and later he said it was sure exciting bouncing along on the road with four hooves making passes at him.

Horse Traders Are Born, Not Made

When we were kids, most of us had horses available. Even a few town kids had them, including Lawrence Laugenesse. He would come to my place on Saturday and help clean barns and do chores in order to have someone to ride with in the afternoon.

Lawrence was a big time operator. He was always trading horses or cars, but generally his trades needed extra cash. I can remember going with Lawrence in the back door of the Cold Storage Meat Market, where Books Etc. in Livingston is now located, grabbing a couple weenies out of the smoke house, and looking for his dad to furnish twenty bucks or so "boot" for a trade. Many years later, Bob Zander expressed Lawrence's passion perfectly. "I'd rather trade horses than make an honest dollar any day."

CAREFUL INSTRUCTIONS ARE CRUCIAL

Most of these stories are my own but Dutch VanOrden told one at coffee this morning that I feel fits into this chapter. His brother-in-law Kenny Killorn was helping bring in cattle from summer range. The lady of the ranch fixed a good lunch, and in as much as Kenny had the only saddle with bags, she put the lunch in them. Getting all the stock together out of all the draws and gullies took a little longer than expected. About 3 o'clock, the crew finally all got together and was ready for lunch. But there was none. Poor Kenny didn't know it was for everyone; he thought everyone had a lunch of their own, and he'd eaten everything in his saddle bags.

Horses and people, put them together, and there will always be stories. I'll bet there are a million of them since Park County got its start.

CHAPTER FIVE

GROWING UP

I would suppose that kids were pretty much the same when I was one as they are now. However, I do not remember the dilemma facing the young today of not having anything to do. Our problem was there were some things to do before we could do what we wanted to do. I think part of the problem is that kids today do things too early and have used up all the kid thrills by the time they are 12. Examples of this is learning to swim and riding a bicycle. Most kids get swimming lessons when they are two or three years old, and most can ride a bike before first grade. Mark Fox had a bicycle repair shop in the alley on the end of 6th Street. He was a two-wheeler man. He had one of those old bikes with a big front wheel and a little bitty one in back. He would always ride this bike in the Fourth of July parade, and it was already an antique in the thirties. He also rode a regular bike, and when he went motorized, he had an old Harley Davidson. If he took his wife with him, it was in a side car on the motorcycle. Repairing bikes was a part-time job for Mark, his real vocation being a machinist in a shop. He started his bike business in the 1920s, and he once told me that, when he started, all his business was with men; then it moved down to high school age kids, then to grade school kids, and before he died, he was repairing bikes for preschoolers.

Most of the kids I knew learned bike riding in about third or fourth grade. It only took about a block or two to learn at that age. To find a bike to learn on was the problem. Now you see anxious parents running around the block holding the seat of a little bike with a three- or four-year-old. After learning to ride, I found a used bike for three bucks, but it didn't have a chain. I wheeled it down to Mark Fox's and got a used chain. I was in business, and it's the only time I can remember three solid days of rain in this country. But I didn't care—I rode and rode.

YELLOWSTONE PARK BY BICYCLE

I still had that same bike when Bill and Wes Strong and I rode our bikes through Yellowstone Park. We did that the summer Bill and I got out of the eighth grade and Wes, out of the seventh.

My dad hauled us to Gardiner, and we took off up Mammoth Hill and got as far as Norris campground the first day (a distance of roughly 20 miles). We each had one blanket, some grub, and a little cooking gear—we were traveling in class! After supper, it was dark, and with one blanket on the ground and two over the top, we all crawled into the same bed. We must have been tired because we didn't wake very early; the camp was alive with people, and our clothes were on a table about 10 feet from the bed. With just our underwear on, we had to make a dash for our clothing, and after that we learned to dress under the covers.

There were many bears at that time, and campers tied their food in a bag and hung it between two trees, presumably high enough so bears couldn't reach it. We did this at the Canyon campground, then rolled our bed out under it, and went to sleep. Our food and cooking gear were scattered around in the morning. I don't know how a bear could have swatted that sack down without hitting our bed with it, but if it did we didn't know it.

Other than springing the frame on my three dollar bike by getting a rope into the sprocket and getting a nice guy to bend it back, the only excitement was coming down the hill on the road from Mt. Washburn to Tower Falls. Our bikes didn't have brakes on front and back, only a coaster brake on the back wheel. This brake got so hot it was smoking. We each wore out a pair of shoes holding them against the front tire trying to slow down. What fun! The last day was the frosting on the cake—from Mammoth to Livingston and nearly all downhill.

SUMMERTIME, AND THE LIVIN'S EASY...

Swimming was a little tougher, me being a slow learner. But when it finally happened, it was full ahead from there. We had a great swimming hole in Billman Creek right where RY Lumber is now.

It was fairly deep in the middle, and it had a little current and a little sandy spot to lay on.

Next came the river, swimming across and then having to walk barefoot upstream to swim back to the approximate spot you started. After that was making rafts and floating on inner tubes.

WINTER ADVENTURES

Winter was always a great time. First, it was sleds, and then it was making skis out of barrel staves. We would cut a leather strap out of the top of an old boot and nail the toe strap to the stave. A refinement was to cut rubber bands from an inner tube and put this under your shoe toe and against the strap and then around the back of your heel… man's first ski bindings. We started on the creek bank and soon graduated to the big draws on the Wineglass. These were fairly long runs, and by the time we reached high school age, we had real skis. We would carry them clear to the timber line on the Wineglass and ski the draws all the way down. This made only one run per day, but it was about two miles long.

PROCURING CHRISTMAS TREES

We started furnishing the family Christmas tree in about the third or fourth grade. The first time my mom let me go, she told the other kids, "Don't you let him use the axe as he'll chop his leg off." My mom had confidence in me.

The other guys already had their tree and were halfway down the mountain while I was still beavering away with that dull axe. Between chopping and breaking off the last part, I finally felled my first tree and was off down the mountain. We must have had to drag them two or three miles. Probably, there weren't many needles left, but I don't remember that part.

WHEELS

Very few kids had cars in high school, but most of them could drive quite young. My last day of 8th grade, my mother took me to school and let me drive. However, I don't remember getting a driver's license until I was probably a junior or senior in high school. And then there was no test—just 50 cents, and one was made out to you sans photo or social security number.

With very few cars, lots of kids rode bikes in high school. If you didn't have your bike and were skipping a study hall, we'd just borrow one off the bike rack. Of course, we generally brought them back. However, if your bike was missing when you came out to get it, it was just a matter of walking down to Wilcoxsin's or the Super Cream, and it would be leaning on a light post there. This was a very accepted practice with no one getting too upset about it. There must have been a bike stolen once in a while, but I do not remember any.

Work First

Living on a small farm put some serious constrains on all of the above entertainments. There was always corn to hoe, irrigating water to change, or a shed to clean. By high school, I was stacking loose hay and even getting an occasional job driving stacker horse or shocking grain. My first real job was herding cows for a dairy on 9th Street island. I would bring them across the 9th Street bridge and drive them around the waterworks lawn; then it was all open south of Fleshman Creek where the hospital and all those houses are now. The pay was 50 cents a day, and that was a pretty good wage for a ten-year-old.

Making A Dime In The Good, Old Days

Some twenty or thirty years ago, George Senter, an old schoolmate, visited me at my store. He asked me if I remembered when we were in the gopher business. It was a little vague, but he brought it back to me. It went like this. Tom Schwanke would hire George for a dime to pull his little wagon out to my house. Then Tom would pay me a dime for the gophers I caught that day. George would haul the gophers back to 9th Street where a man named John Thealander raised mink in his back yard. Tom would sell the gophers for mink feed and get about 50 cents for his efforts. Looking back, George felt we had been taken advantage of, while I wasn't even aware of the end transaction, so had lived in blissful ignorance.

HAULING MANURE

Believe it or not, one of my favorite jobs was hauling manure. It wasn't the manual labor involved that intrigued me, but the fact that I could drive an old Dodge truck to do the job. This led to quite a profitable business. Many town people had gardens and wanted manure for their gardens and even to put on their lawns. Lawn manure had to be almost free of straw, and sheep manure was the preferred stuff for lawns. It was a short season, but two or three bucks a load took the edge off before getting a summer job.

EDUCATION & INCENTIVE

My dad's education was somewhat limited, and most of his English speaking was learned on his own. This put a tremendous pressure on us kids, especially me, as he felt education was one of the very important things in life. One of his unique approaches to foster this was to invite each of our teachers to a Sunday dinner. This behooved us to be on our good behavior in school as sometime during the school, year my dad would be inquiring about our school activities face to face. Dad didn't just ask questions; he also imparted advice. Part of the advice he would give the teacher was this: "If you ever have to give that kid a licking to straighten him out, just let me know, and he will get another one at home." This provided me with the incentive to have a good report card about every other time. After a bad one, it was get up early and help with the milking of cows and other chores. Then after a good card, things would relax a little, and I could sleep in again. The problem was I had a short memory.

A Visit To The Homestead

I remember only one trip to my grandparents' homestead as a kid. I was there at least a couple days. This is where I first saw real farming; they were hauling wheat bundles with teams into the thrashing machine. The thrasher was powered by a big engine with a long belt connecting it. My most vivid memory is of the men coming in for the noon meal. The teams were all unhitched and fed. The younger bucks would bring their horses in, riding Roman style—one foot on the rump of each horse and steering them with the wrapped-up reins. My uncle Joe was one of these showoffs.

The Rear View Mirror

Travel was limited in those 1930 years. I had an aunt in Bozeman, so we occasionally went there as a family for Sunday dinner. I must have been about 14 before ever getting to Billings, and then it was for showing some lambs as a 4-H club project. Billings was a big town. There must have been fifteen or twenty thousand people at that time! During high school years, I would look at the Greyhound bus when it stopped at the Park Hotel. My dream was to get on that bus and just go anywhere. With the war just around the corner, my wish soon came true. Lots of travel after that, but Livingston looked better on each return. I have thanked God many times for letting me be born in this wonderful place.

All in all, what a great time to grow up and what a great place to do it! I think we can match or beat the kids today with goofy stunts like riding horses or bikes into the river, playing Indian, or breathing into each other's faces to catch the mumps for an easy week out of school. But I don't remember ever being bored.

CHAPTER SIX

FAMILY

I would be totally remiss if I did not explain how my family settled in Park County. My parents were both emigrants, arriving in the USA in the early 1900s. Both were born in Switzerland, but came from two different areas and did not meet until they were adults.

Mom's Side Of The Family

My mother, Mathilda A. Meister, was born March 26, 1900, in Woolerah, Switzerland, and came to the new land with her family—Joe and Mathilda Meister and three brothers, none of whom were school age. The family did not immediately settle in Montana, however, but in Saskatchewan, Canada. Granddad homesteaded in Canada before sending for the rest of his family to come over. My mother's early recollection is getting off the train at Havre, Montana, probably about 1903 or 1904. My grandmother put all their luggage on a pile and had the four kids hold hands around it while she went to buy something to eat. I never did hear whether Granddad was late in picking them up or why he didn't meet the train… perhaps the team and wagon were slower than he anticipated.

The family lived in Canada a couple years, but Granddad wanted to live closer to the mountains. He had relatives in Montana's Sweetgrass County, between Melville and Rapelje. However, he didn't have the money to move his family so he went to the San Francisco area for nearly a year to make enough to move. He hand-milked cows for a large dairy during this period. It must have been rather primitive by today's standards. Cows were milked in a corral, and Granddad said about one third of them had to be roped and tied to a post to make them stand. If someone didn't show up for work, Granddad would milk two strings of 30 cows each.

In 1906, when the family finally arrived in Sweetgrass County and settled in the Gibson area, most homesteads had been taken up so Granddad purchased a relinquishment from Jake Kaiserman. Kaiserman had filed his homestead but not finished proving up on the land. To prove up on land there were various requirements, part of which was to break the sod and farm a portion of it, to build a habitable structure, and to actually reside on the property. After buying the relinquishment, Granddad finished the requirements for having the land deeded to himself.

DAD'S SIDE OF THE FAMILY

My father's name was Gottfried Shellenberg. He was born March 12, 1887, in Hori, Switzerland. Dad was about 20 when he came to the States, and when he was naturalized, he changed his first name to Fred G. Shellenberg. He came with another young man who settled near Grass Range, Montana.

Dad went to Canada for a year or two before coming back to the States to attend a mechanic school in Chicago.

After that, he took a job with Holt Caterpillar Company of Spokane. This was the beginning of the Caterpillar Company of today. These early tractors had crawler tracks in back but had a steering wheel and wheels in front. Dad traveled for the company and apparently showed new owners how to maintain and run their tractors.

WEDDING BELLS & LIVINGSTON

Dad was working with these tractors at Glass Lindsey Lake, which is some east of Big Timber, Montana, toward Melville. This is where my mother and dad met; they were married in 1922 in Big Timber—Dad was 35, and Mom was 22. My dad must have quit the tractor company, as he ran a livery stable in Big Timber for a short time before moving to Livingston. I was born August 21, 1923, in Livingston.

Fred G. Shellenberg and his Harley in 1910.

Fred G. Shellenberg with a Holt Caterpillar, circa 1920.

MONTANA POWER

This part of my history is pure conjecture, but I think that, while Dad worked in the Big Timber area, he met Jake Kaiserman, the same man that Granddad Meister purchased his homestead from. Mr. Kaiserman was manager of the electric power company in Big Timber. During this period, Montana Power was purchasing and consolidating small power companies. Mr. Kaiserman became the manager of the Livingston division of Montana Power, and he offered my dad a job at the head gates of the power generating facility.

At that time, the Livingston division of Montana Power generated its own power with a system of dams, canals, and a power plant where the Edgewater apartment complex on the end of 10th Street now stands. My dad was a dam keeper, and we lived in a company house at the head gates. The head gates were about halfway between Livingston and the canyon south of town.

The main dam was located at the warm springs about a mile downstream from Carters Bridge. Dad worked on the dam and canals but was on call most of the time to increase or decrease the flow to the power plant. This system was all a manual operation with a system of channeling water from the canal back into the river if they needed less flow at the power station. A crank telephone was the communication system for changing the water flow.

The back of the house we lived in was straight down to water, and there were two bridges to it—one over the main canal and

Fred G. Shellenberg with his wife Mathilda and his son Fred, circa 1925.

This was the power plant that was at the end of 10th Street. The arches at the bottom of the build are millraces where the water flows back to the river after going through the turbines.

one over the spillway canal. Then there was a road between the main canal and the river that went clear to town. This was a company road, and I can remember the work crews with team and wagon coming to work on the dams. Sam Barrett was one of the early workers I remember. He had been at Cokedale before the coal mining closed down and he moved to Livingston. He also lived in a company house, which was later remodeled and became Dr. Pearson's beautiful river home on the end of 12th Street.

EARLY MEMORIES

Montana Power closed its power plant in 1928. We moved from the house at the head gates to our place on the five-acre tracts that year just before I started first grade. But as young as I was, I remember many incidents from the head gates. I can remember carrying notes for my mother to Bill Strong's mother, who lived on the river about half way from the head gates to the power plant. I remember the threat of dire punishment if I went close to the water, and there was water everywhere. When I crossed a bridge, I had to walk in the middle and never close to the edge. I was allowed to get the mail from our mail box on the Park Road, and while getting the mail, a Mr. Charlie Bruckert would stop his team of mules to rest them. He worked for the highway department and graded the gravel road from Livingston to Carter's Bridge with mules and an old pull grader.

I can remember my mother fishing under a yard light in front of the house. The canal was about 20 feet from the house. Mom sold the trout to the Cold Storage Meat Market. It was legal then, and as I remember that they were good size, in the two-pound range. After the power plant shut down, the water ceased to flow down the main canal. There was a large apron or spillway where the water flowed over into the canal. There was a hole at the end of the spillway, and this hole had water in it for some time after the flow was stopped. I was playing down by the spillway one day and noticed the hole was filled with fish. I told my mother I could catch lots of fish and to give me a bucket. After much crabbing at her for a bucket, she finally gave me a five-pound lard bucket. I came back with the head of about a 12-inch trout stuck into the bucket and holding his tail with the other hand. Mom came to life then, and we filled a wash tub with fine trout, catching them by hand in that shallow pond. That day, all the neighbors and the Montana Power crew were supplied with fish.

FAMILY ADDITIONS

By the time we moved from the head gates in 1928, our family had increased by a brother, Arthur William who was born April 23, 1926, and a baby sister, Evelyn Marie, who was born September 12, 1927. We called Evelyn "Sister" while my brother Art was re-named—by Bill Olson, the Power Company line foreman—"Ole, the big Swede" with just "Ole" for short. My next sister, Anna Barbara, was born on February 27, 1930, and was for some reason called "Tootsie." The baby of the family, my brother John Henry, was born on January 15, 1935, and was simply always called John—no imagination! The use of these nicknames continued for quite a few years with even the neighbor kids using them. One day my father decided no more nicknames. This was a very difficult change until he instigated a nickel fine each time we slipped. My dad found we could be fast learners with the proper incentive.

COMPANY MEMORIES

After moving to the five-acre tracts, Dad continued to work for Montana Power. He liked the work, and the company was very good to him and our family. Then Dad contracted TB and died in 1943 at the TB sanitarium at Galen. I believe the company paid his wages until he died and then helped my mother get her social security benefit until all her kids were out of school.

The period of time that Dad worked at the head gates and then for the company in town was somewhat of a transition period. Montana Power was still using horses for the crews and some trucks. One horse that endeared itself to the service crew would run away when an electric spark occurred. Generally, it would stay on the street and run to the barn. On the north side of the railroad tracks, however, it would not seek out the crossing or underpass but would head straight for the barn, crossing the tracks at the most convenient place. All that would be left of the buggy would be the shafts. With that practical joking crew, this was just good fun.

The first Power Company office I was familiar with was on Second Street, about where the First Interstate parking lot is now. The next building north was the Strand Theatre. In the basement of the Strand, A.W. Miles Company had a large steam-heating plant, which heated the Strand and a few other buildings on that side of the street. The steam was also piped across the street and heated the entire Park Hotel block and all Miles stores on Second Street. A.W. Miles had hardware, women's clothing, and groceries in a row on Second Street. The A.W. Miles Company also had a lumber and coal company between D and E Streets on Park, and it had a farm machinery business that had outlets in Livingston, Wilsall, and Big Timber. A.W. was a nephew of General Nelson Miles, who helped subdued most of the hostile Indians after the Custer fracas.

My brother Art worked for Montana Power after World War II until retirement, and now his son Jeff works for the company. My brother started with the company in Helena; Jake Kaiserman was his first manager… Rather strange how one man, Jake Kaiserman, could touch the lives of both sides as well as three generations of my family over a period of nearly 50 years.

I only worked for the Power Company for about six months before going into the service in 1942. I read meters, generally traveling at a full gallop. I would finish my route for the day by two o'clock, which gave me the opportunity to visit with the office crew or the line crews, help out on various jobs, and run errands. I even met the president of the company, Mr. Buck. He shook my hand and told me he'd started with the company reading meters.

Bert Cutler

One of the Montana Power service men I particularly remember was Bert Cutler. He was soft spoken and pleasant, and he would be considered "laid back" in today's lingo. Bert's personal car was always a late vintage Buick, and he kept it immaculate. His pickup, however, was another story. Most of the fenders were just hanging on. When Bert was in reverse, he rarely looked back. While Bert was backing out of the shop one day, Bill Olson, the line crew foreman, hit the back of Bert's pickup with a shovel. Bert never looked around, just pulled ahead, and tried for the garage door opening with a new angle of approach.

Whispering Holmes

Meade "Whispering" Holmes was a lineman and service man both. He wasn't a large man, but he could beller like a bull… hence the nickname. He was my Cub Scout leader, and his commanding voice came in handy with about 25 or 30 kids. I do not remember him having any help even on a camp out. One time, while we were camping out, Bill and Wes Strong and I were in a pup tent with the rest of the kids in tents of various sizes and some of them just sleeping on the ground. Things just would not settle down after dark with whooping and hollering and pulling up of tent stakes. Finally, our little pup tent collapsed on top of us, and we came crawling out. Mr. Holmes yelled, "Don't put it back up!

Just throw it into the pickup! I'm taking you home."

Man, that put the fear in us! We conspired that, when he took us home, we were not going into our houses but putting in the night outdoors somewhere. We knew it would be "Hail Columbia" with our parents. But our good old scout master just took us down the road a hundred yards or so and helped put up our tent, with the instruction we could come back in the morning IF we could behave ourselves. This little action, of course, made believers out of the rest of the camp, and things really settled down for the night. The next morning, it was business as usual.

Montana Power... what a great bunch of guys and what a great company. When things were slow and tough for the Power Company during the 1930s, there wasn't a lay off. They kept all the workers on at half-time. This kept the wolf from the door until things picked up. The company in Livingston furnished doctor and hospital for employees and their families under a local agreement with Dr. Windsor and the Park Hospital. I do not know if the company did this in other towns, but I suppose they did. In the late thirties, the employees of the company unionized. My dad was a laborer (a grunt), but was opposed to the idea. He, of course, joined when the union was voted in.

Then came the big adventure of World War Two.

Shellenberg siblings about 1936. Fred horseback. On fence, L to R: Anna, Art, & Evelyn.

Fred G. & Mathilda Shellenberg's family. L to R: Mathilda holding John Henry, Anna Barbara, Arthur William, Evelyn Marie, Fred G., & Fred Joseph. This photo was taken in the summer or fall of 1935. "Dad sent this photo to family in Switzerland to show his success story— a barn, an automobile, and five kids!"

CHAPTER SEVEN

WORLD WAR II

My start in the military was with a lie, and though I have never regretted doing it, I have never been proud of the lie itself. In 1937, I enlisted in the Livingston Howitzer Company of the Montana National Guard when I was 14. We wore campaign hats, like Smokey Bear, riding britches with wrap leggings, and a pistol holster on a web belt… mighty heady stuff for a 14-year-old, even if he only weighed 115 pounds or thereabouts. We didn't have to show a birth certificate, and lots of the guys were underage. We had an experienced batch of officers, however; some of them were veterans of World War One. Captain Buck Wheat was company commander, with Lieutenants "Duck" White and Mazel VanOrden. The top sergeant was Ray Shadoan. Ray had a stubborn-looking lantern jaw and truly looked the part of a top kick. Our supply sergeant was Rudy Hicks, who probably had the most service time. He was practically a fixture and the only full time employ of the Guard in Livingston. He even lived at the Civic Center where the supply room and drills were held.

ONE DOLLAR A DRILL

We drilled on Tuesday and Thursday evenings during winter months, and privates pay was one dollar a drill. The first two years of my hitch, we had summer camp in Helena. Camp was fun and busy. We would have close-order drill, some time on the rifle range, and a long march of 8 or 10 miles for an overnight bivouac. I was referred to as "98 pounds soaking wet." One of the officers even offered to carry my full pack, which consisted of a blanket, one-half of a pup tent, eating utensils, and personal effects. I refused the kind offer and found the little skinny guys really could do better on a long, hot march than the big ones. As the army has always done, we marched for 50 minutes and then had a 10-minute break. One time we were on a country road with the battalion taking the break by sitting in the barrow pit. Many of the other company's men had headed for a nearby farmhouse to refill their canteens at an outdoor pump. It was our first break. Captain Wheat yelled, "Stand fast!" when a few of our men started taking off for water. "Any Howitzer company man that can't make it on one canteen of water gets the belt line with buckles when we get back." I don't remember ever swinging the buckle end, but while half the battalion was scrounging for water at every stop, not a man from Howitzer Company left ranks.

Now the belt line was a rite, whereby the company would

Private Fred Shellenberg stands second from the left in the second row from the back. The guns are a 37-mm Howitzer and a 3-inch mortar.

form in two lines facing each other, all having a leather garrison belt to administer a good swat to any recipient running the line. Normally the men that ran this gauntlet were those that had received a promotion during the year. This included commissioned and non-commissioned officers, and this practice gave the men a chance to give some deserving sergeant a good whack.

Practical Jokes

My age and size provided considerable entertainment for some of the older heads. On one occasion, a batch of them was playing poker on a camp cot in my squad tent. One of them said, "These cards are getting raggy. Shellenberg, go get the card stretcher."

"Where is it, Sarge?"

"Where do you think? In the orderly tent, on the double." I ran to the orderly tent, which is the office for the top sergeant and the company officers. I was informed there that the card stretcher had been loaned to A Company. I ran over there and was told they had returned it to our supply tent. The supply sergeant sent me on to the kitchen. The kitchen was Oliver Ebert, our first cook's domain. Now Oliver was generally a good-natured, joke-loving guy, but he also had a reputation of being one tough hombre. It was rumored that he could knock a man down and hit him twice more before he hit the ground. When I asked him for the non-existent card stretcher, Oliver sat me down and began telling me the facts of life, ending with the admonition, "If any of those guys push you around too much, let me know, and I'll straighten them out." Then he gave me a donut, and I don't just remember for sure, but he might have patted me on the head. Ah, life in the peace-time army.

FT. LEWIS

The third and last camp on this hitch was a real bang-up affair at Ft. Lewis, Washington. We rode the train both ways. That camp at Ft. Lewis was the last of the old army. We were infantry, but there were cavalry and artillery battalions there also. During the large "passing in review" of the entire camp, the horse artillery passed the review stand at a full gallop. The guns and ammunition wagons were all dead axle, and the soldiers had to sit on the axle between the wheel and the ammo boxes, with arms folded, looking straight ahead until, "Present Arms," and they held a hand salute passing the reviewing stand. When the horse cavalry passed, my position didn't give me a view so I don't know if they passed the stand at a gallop or a walk, but I presume a gallop as that would be much more impressive and exciting.

That was the year 1940, and war clouds were gathering. When we returned to Livingston, Lieutenant White called me and several other underage guys together and told us we were out of the service unless we could prove our age. We were let out. I do not remember getting a discharge but I do remember that White assured us it would not be dishonorable so we must have gotten one.

THE MILK BUSINESS

After finishing high school in 1941, I worked delivering milk for the Marigold Dairy owned by Jim Roark. Jim always said a good milkman should be able to carry three bottles of milk in each hand and jump a three-foot fence without dropping them. Although we did deliver some milk to stores and restaurants, most of it was delivered directly to homes. Part of the job was going to the farms to pick up bulk milk. We bottled it in a little plant on the back of a lot on South C Street. Pasteurized milk was just coming in, and most of our customers used raw milk, and we bought the pasteurized stuff at the Farmers Creamery. Once in a while, Jim would just "pasteurize in the truck" by taking off the raw milk caps and replacing them with pasteurized milk caps!

AND THEN I GOT A HARLEY

It was during this time I bought a Harley Davidson motorcycle, 74 cubic inches. We weren't measuring in CCs, and with a megaphone muffler, that thing would really rumble. Then I worked for Montana Power, reading meters for about six months. But with a motor cycle, the town couldn't hold me. I rode to Olympia, Washington, and got work there in an automotive parts house. Then Pearl Harbor was bombed on December 7, 1941.

ENLISTING & WAITING

My dad wrote me a letter, asking me to come home if I was going to enlist, which is what I did. I enlisted in the Army Air Corps for pilot training. This meant I had to wait for a new group to be formed. While sitting around home waiting for my call, I drove my mother crazy, power-diving a chair or simulating other acts of flying in various ways.

While waiting, Bill and Wes Strong and I went to Toole, Utah, to work construction. Going down, we were reasonably broke so we decided to cut down on expenses. The agreement was we would go easy on breakfast, settling for coffee and a donut, and would only have one big meal a day. The first morning we lined up at the lunch counter. When asked for his order, Bill said, "Coffee and a donut." I said, "Coffee and a donut." Wes broke the monotony with, "Ham and eggs, please."

On arriving in Utah, we found jobs to be plentiful and wages good. Most jobs were six or seven days a week with good overtime. We worked at Toole for about a month and, between the three of us, operated nearly every piece of equipment Chemical Contractors had to offer.

This is the result of being farm boys and being eager to fill in everywhere. There were nearly always vacancies of workers on each shift; hence, we drove various trucks and Cats and even operated the batch plant. One evening, I rode to the construction camp with the steel foreman. He offered to teach me the steel business and keep me out of the service for the entire war. "No, thanks," I replied. "I'm awaiting a call now." I had big worries. I was afraid the war would be over before I could get into the army. After I did get in, the worry was it would be over before I could get overseas. After I got overseas, the worry reversed, and I was afraid it would never get over with! While I was waiting to be called, one day my mother told me, "You won't be a pilot."

"Why not, Mom?"

"Because you're too careless." She had me pegged, right down to the eyeballs. After cadet preflight training at San Antonio, Texas, and then primary flight training in Pine Bluff, Arkansas, I flunked my very first check ride. The check pilot asked for a stall straight ahead, which I gave him with enthusiasm. The problem was that, to do a stall, one had to clear the area with a 90-degree turn in each direction to make sure there were no other aircraft under you or near you. Having failed to do this, I was immediately washed out as a pilot.

WASHED-OUT PILOTS

After being thrown in with hundreds and maybe thousands of washed out pilots, we finally deduced this was the Air Corps method of recruiting gunners. Gunners, in addition to manning the 50-caliber machine guns on bombers, were either engineers, radiomen, or armourers. I was sent to radio school.

It was a crash course. We learned repair, presumably; Morse code, ten words a minute; how to conduct ourselves; and how to use proper procedure when transmitting and receiving. It was general consensus at the school that a good radioman was somewhat screwy, a little off beat. I found this to be essentially true with nearly everyone but myself.

Next stop was Yuma, Arizona, for gunnery school. This was learning the operation of turrets and various gun positions, air to air gunnery, shooting at a towed target, and air to ground practice on ground targets from about 500 feet altitude. This was the most fun. As a sidelight, during my army career, I managed to shoot expert with every weapon except the one I was assigned to, which was the 50-caliber machine gun. After gunnery school, we received our silver wings. There was even a popular song during the war: "He wears a pair of silver wings." Along with an issued pair of Ray-Ban sunglasses and those wings, we were wheels, almost showoffs.

Then we were assigned to air crews for final crew training. I met my crew at Muroc Army Airbase, which is now Edwards Air Force Base. This was on the desert, with no weather problems, and we flew night and day missions, with each member of the crew learning what they were responsible for.

Three Musketeers. L to R: Wes Strong, Fred Shellenberg, & Bill Strong.

YOUNG & RECKLESS

These crews were young and reckless. Most of the men, even pilots were 23 years old or younger. I recall viewing a training movie telling crews, especially pilots, what not to do. The "do nots" included not flying under bridges or power lines and maintaining at least 500 feet of altitude, even on air to ground gunnery exercises. One of the pilots was quite expansive and told his crew, "That's fun! We're going to do that." On the first air ground gunnery mission, he flew low enough to hit a large cactus with the bottom of the aircraft fuselage, tearing loose a bomb bay door, which was dangling in the slip stream. He wondered if his engineer could fix it before landing!

PILOT

Our pilot, however, was 28 and married with one child. When we got overseas, we used to brag about him because he was careful and didn't scare the daylights out of you like some. Lt. Daryl Mason—good pilot and an absolute straight arrow. He flew by the book, always prudent, but he also flew over the middle of the target, not around the edge where things were easier.

CO-PILOT

Lt. Stan Burda from New Jersey was our co-pilot. He was a very laid back guy. About halfway through our missions, we nicknamed him "15 Degrees Landing Gear." One day, when the pilot asked for 15 degrees of flaps to slow down air speed, Stan hit the wrong lever and dropped the landing gear. After getting to Italy, Stan bought himself an accordion and decided to be a professional musician after the war, and he did have a polka band in the late forties and fifties after being discharged. Stan had a very disciplined approach to music. When we weren't flying, his day was split into two hours of doing scales, two hours of playing what he liked, two hours of new stuff that he was learning, and then the final reward of two hours of requests from anyone that was still in earshot.

Navigator

Our navigator was a brain and always knew where he was. When we flew from Newfoundland to the Azores, the islands appeared dead ahead, not off to one side—this after an eight-hour flight over all water. On bombing missions, the entire group flew using only the lead ship navigation. The other navigators kept track in case they were separated from the group. Lt. Arnwine frequently would comment on the lead navigator, "How can he navigate in a circle?" Apparently, navigation was conducted along straight lines.

Bombardier

Our bombardier was Lt. Germer. He was another easy-going character, but he was careful of his handling of the bombsight. The Nordon Bombsight was the only thing on the plane classified as secret. Part of this sight utilized calcite, which was mined near Springdale,

Montana, in Park County. Again, the entire formation dropped bombs on the lead bombardier's instructions. Germer was lead only once, when the lead plane was disabled and we moved into that position. We all had our fingers crossed, but Germer hit dead on, and the entire 456th Bomb Group dropped on our lead.

Engineer

The rest of the crew was made up of enlisted men. We all made either staff or tech sergeant during our tour. Walter Krawczyk was our engineer. He didn't quite finish high school to enlist. While the rest of us knot heads were reading funny books or playing cards, he was reading tech manuals on the B24 airplane. He was the only flight engineer I knew that was ever asked by the ground crew to help change out an engine or work on the hydraulics or electrical parts. He could be rather short with officers on occasion, but always being in the right, he managed to get away with it.

Ball Gunner

Our ball gunner was Leon MacLaughlin. He was a little guy that fit perfectly into that ball hanging out of the belly of the airplane. He was small, but his ego was large. He was funny and assertive and the only one of the crew that became a pro and did something over 20 years in the service.

Armourer

Our armourer and one of the waist gunners was Jefferson; I can't remember his first name as everyone called him Jeff. He was another old guy, the oldest I knew except for a few senior officers. I believe he was 30 when we got overseas. He was a very stabilizing influence on the crew, including officers, even if he did treat us as adolescents.

Tail Gunner

Our tail gunner was Dick Weins. He didn't train with our crew but was assigned in San Francisco where we went to pick up a new B24. Our first tail gunner at Muroc went AWOL. We were assigned another named Pfluger. We got along great, but he came down sick in San Francisco, and when time waits for no one, he was left for sick call. Weins had been left by the crew he trained with for the same reason so he was assigned to us. In today's parlance, he was not a happy camper. He missed his own crew and felt we were a bunch of eight balls. After a few weeks, however, he fit in like a glove. I recall one of our first missions when the pilot was doing an oxygen check. We flew at altitudes that required being on oxygen. The check was to make sure a hose wasn't accidently detached and someone had passed out. Everyone checked in but Weins. A man was sent back to find what the problem was. He was okay. His microphone and headset were disconnected, not the oxygen.

When he got back on, his reassurance was, "What are you worried about? I only foul up in extreme emergencies."

A squad tent is square and tall enough to walk around in except at the edges. The sidewalls are about four feet high, and the ceiling comes to a peak in the center from all four sides. Each tent is designed for eight people, but with only six enlisted men on a crew, we had adequate room. However, many of the crews, including ours, elaborated on the design of the tents by extending the side walls outward, which in turn extended the roof. Then we hired Italians to make a four-foot stone wall to replace the canvas tent walls that had been extended. This presented another engineering problem. With the canvas walls extended, there was an opening to the sky in each corner. You could build the stone walls with the corner following the canvas sides, or you could build square and patch in canvas on the open corners. By patching in canvas, you ended up with a larger floor space, and being Americans, we of course needed all the space we could get. The weather was so good I just never got around to patching in a piece of canvas on my corner. But one morning there was six inches of snow on the foot of my cot! Good old Chuck Mead helped me patch in and weather proof my corner.

Nose Gunner

Our nose gunner was Chuck Mead. Today we would nickname him Mr. Clean or Mr. Fixit. He made life very livable in our squad tent. He installed running water, utilizing a wing tank for water storage and half of an oxygen storage bottle for a sink. He also built a stove from half an oil drum with another wing tank in the olive tree for fuel oil. All of the crew except Weins and myself had wooden floors made from bomb crates. Dick and I felt the good earth was sufficient. However, one afternoon Chuck came running in with news. "The so-and-so crew had been shot down. Supply has picked up all their personal gear, and we'd better get you guys a section of floor before it's gone!" So Weins and I moved up in the world.

Radioman

The last guy on the crew was the radioman, myself, no less. I did know how to turn the set off and on but, other than in training, I had no occasion to use it. We maintained radio silence on missions, even voice between aircraft. After bombs away, the lead radioman would use CW transmission to notify the group "Mission accomplished." I did that one time when Germer dropped the bombs.

Krawczyk was always a little leery of me after a little incident in training. We were on a night mission. I was doodling away, drawing a spark gap with a lead pencil from a loaded antenna. I could draw a spark nearly an inch. Krawczyk noticed it and flipped. "Are you trying to blow us up?" Sparks are not conducive to safety in an aircraft that was prone to gas leaks in the bomb bay.

Then, trying to be a little more attentive, I noticed the cowling on number two engine was red hot and called Krawczyk's attention to this. He couldn't understand what I was talking about; when he finally figured it out, he informed me that it was a red light between the fuselage and the engine reflecting off the cowling.

Later when flying from Africa to Italy, we landed at an almost deserted field to get our final orders. I presume the pilot got those orders by voice from somewhere. We were going to start up the engines again, but there wasn't anyone around to stand fire guard during start up. Normally there was always a ground crewman with a fire extinguisher to hit a flaming exhaust with CO_2 if needed. I grabbed a two-pound extinguisher and told Krawczyk I'd do it. He started explaining the extinguisher to me. All the thanks he got from me was, "What do you think I am? Stupid?"

The first engine started up fine as I examined the extinguisher. It was red and had a sort of tapered funnel alongside of it. I thought, now if this funnel is straight out instead of alongside, I will be more ready in case of need. I moved the funnel around… which set off the extinguisher. I quickly turned it back, but after breaking the seal, there was no stopping it, and the CO_2 emptied out. Krawczyk was furious, and I ran all around that air strip trying to find someone with a new extinguisher, but no luck. We finally took off without one, and things were rather tense. However, he eventually forgave me, and Walt and I still keep in touch. He has visited me in Montana, and I have visited him twice in Indian Orchard, Massachusetts. On his Christmas card this year, his wife said he retired once, but the plant called him back. He is now 77 and thinking of retiring again. He's probably still reading tech manuals on the equipment.

TRAINING ON THE DESERT

During our time on the California desert, I don't remember much about the training, but I remember quite a few memories from the times we had weekends off. We used a limousine service to get from the desert to the Los Angeles area. What wheels! We didn't ride buses like the common people. I don't think we really swaggered with our Ray-Ban sunglasses on, but I'm sure we came mighty close to it.

I spent one weekend with MacLaughlin at his mother's cabin at Big Bear Lake. One weekend was spent in North Hollywood watching a movie being made at a country club. Another weekend was spent on the beach at Santa Monica, and one weekend I took a pretty girl dancing at the Palladium Ball Room. Somehow I met her in the afternoon and asked her to go with me. She said I could go home with her, and if her dad said it was okay, she would go. I must have passed muster because we had a spaghetti dinner and danced to some big band sounds.

NEW PLANE & NEW UNIFORMS

After crew training, we picked up a brand new airplane in San Francisco. We test flew it with the various positions checking for any deficiencies, which ground crews corrected. At the same time, we were issued brand new flight gear, including a Colt .45 automatic with shoulder holster. Our flight coveralls didn't have pockets on the side but below the knees. It's said that clothes make the man, and that was our garb, including the .45 in shoulder holster, outside, not concealed. Then off for Amarillo, Texas, which was the first stop on our trek overseas. We only stayed overnight, but with mostly recruits on the base, we cut a wide swath.

When Krawczyk and I came back from the PX, we failed to salute a fresh Second Lieutenant. He stopped us with the usual, "Don't you salute an officer?" I saluted, but Krawczyk showed him a tube of toothpaste he was carrying in his saluting hand. The officer told him to put it in the other hand, which he did. Then they both stood there until the officer said, "Well?" Krawczyk finally saluted. As we walked away, Krawczyk said, "The Jeep." Now that was an expression I'd not ever heard before, but it was pure Krawczyk.

Next stop: Granier Field, New Hampshire. I only remember two incidents from there. I walked into the prop wash while the ground crew was running up our engines, and it flipped me into a drainage ditch—lots of wind, like Park County! The other memorable incident had to do with the fact that, for some reason, there was Campbell's Cream of Mushroom soup by the case for sale at the PX. We all bought a case, and most of us started eating it immediately. We ate it cold; we ate it hot when we could find a way to heat it; and we also made sandwiches out of it. About a month after we were settled and flying missions in Italy, Chuck Mead brought out three cans of soup, and we all had a treat. The rest of us had even forgotten there had ever been any. It's possible there was too much else going on to remember soup.

Standing, L to R: Pilot Lt. Daryl Mason, Co-Pilot Lt. Stan Burda, Navigator Lt. Arnwine, & Bombardier Lt. Germer.
Kneeling, L to R: Ball Gunner Leon MacLaughlin, Armourer Jeff Jefferson, Radioman Fred Shellenberg, Nose Gunner Chuck Mead, Engineer Walter Krawczyk, & Tail Gunner Dick Weins.

CHAPTER EIGHT

THE AIR WAR OVER EUROPE

After Granier Field, it was either Goose or Gander, I can't remember which, in Newfoundland; then the Azores; then Marakech, Morocco, and Tunis in Tunisia; and then finally the 745th Bomb Squadron, 456th Bomb Group, 15th Air Force near Fogia, Italy.

A day or two before we arrived was the day of the devastating raid on the Ploesti Oil Fields. This was the first and only time to my knowledge of a low level bombing by B24 heavy bombers. This was done in flights of formations flying over the target at altitudes so low they were flying into the rubble and smoke sent up from planes ahead. The reasoning was that anti-aircraft fire was so great they could fly under it. I don't really know all about it, but nearly half of our group was lost or wrecked their airplanes landing.

LADY PATRICIA

We were welcomed with our brand new B24, which we promptly

named "Lady Patricia" after the pilot's baby daughter. We were soon in the swing of things and started completing our 35 missions, which was the requirement for flight crews to return to the states. Some of the ground personnel felt this was unfair, but they all had the option, even over there, to start flying and do the 35 missions.

We generally started in the dark with a quick breakfast, and then trucks hauled the entire crews to Group Headquarters for briefing. This is when we found out where and what the target was. We soon found out that the huge rail yards in Vienna or any oil field or refinery were hard targets with much anti-aircraft fire. The easy targets, like bridges or little airfields, were called milk runs. Unfortunately, the big targets had to be hit every ten days or two weeks. Those Germans could rebuild things… or at least get them semi-operational very quickly.

Flying Missions

About halfway through our missions, the enlisted men, who were briefed separately, were quite severely reprimanded by a light colonel for occasionally letting off a few rounds of 50-caliber shells while preflighting the airplanes. Gunners would check the operation of the electrical solenoid that activated the trigger on the machine guns. The tail, belly, nose, and upper turrets all had two machine guns. The waist gunners only had one each and fired them manually. When checking these guns, if there was a shell in the barrel or if the ammo belt was connected, the gun would, of course, start firing. The ammunition belt was levered into all the turrets and waist guns, but the ball or belly turret, which used the same system, could also feed in by gravity because the belts were poised over the guns instead of alongside. The colonel warned us, "The next one of you dopes (I may have the wrong word) that lets off a round is going to be court martialed."

After briefing, the crews were trucked back to the planes parked on hardstands—round areas of steel matting material the same as what the taxi strips and runways were constructed of. The ground crew chief would have the put-put (generator) running in preparation for both ground and air crew to preflight the plane. Each crew member would preflight his area of the plane to make sure everything was operational. Mac crawled into his ball turret, dropped it out of its recess, swung it around a few times, and then tested the gun solenoids. Low and behold, that very morning he let off about three rounds, which perforated an empty oil drum beside the hardstand. There were two or three jeeps full of officers there so fast I think they dropped out of the sky. It's the only time I ever saw Mac halfway shook. He even stammered a little. The nice thing about being an enlisted man on an air crew is that we always had a protective covering of four officers that, right or wrong, would immediately go to bat for us. Mac wasn't court martialed, but they sure made a believer out of him.

After everyone was through with preflight, the pilots ran up the engines, making sure they were at full power. The gas trucks would top off the gas tanks, and we'd start watching the tower. Two red flares meant the mission was canceled. One green flare meant start lining up. It was probably one-half to three-quarters of a mile to the end of the runway, depending from which end we were taking off. Each runway or field had four squadrons, which comprised a group. The planes were assigned a takeoff order, which corresponded to their position in the formation. We generally flew number two slot so, although we took off early, we had to circle while everyone else assembled. Then it was off over the Adriatic Sea with four squadrons to a group and groups as far as the eye could see.

Our 456th Bomb Group was commanded by Colonel Steed. The insignia was a colt with wings. The lettering was, "Colonel Steed and his Flying Colts." Our squadron insignia was a sleepy looking lizard or some such animal with miniature bird-like wings to parody the Davis wing design on the B24. The animal's name was "Lardasserous Rex." The fuselage of the B24 was clumsy looking, and they were not pretty on the ground like the tail-dragging B17. However, they could haul more pounds of bombs and had longer range. There were way more B24s than B17s but the news in the states nearly always stated, "B17 Flying Fortresses hammered Europe today."

TAKEOFF

It ran little thrills up and down your spine to see 4 squadrons of eight to fifteen planes each, depending on the number that were serviceable, taxi out for takeoff. They seemed nose heavy on the ground with the nose wheel bouncing every time brakes were applied. I don't remember the interval for takeoff, but it was very rapid, as the squadrons had to assemble and then the group had to be assembled with the four squadrons. These planes were powered with four Pratt & Whitney 1200-horsepower, turbo-supercharged engines. The noise was immense, and each aircraft, after lining up on the runway, ran their engines wide open before releasing the brakes. This was to have enough speed to lift off with a heavy load before running out of runway. Some of the hot shot pilots tried to pull them up before the end of the runway, which caused the plane to slough along trying to pick up speed in the air. Our pilot, Pilot Mason, would use the entire runway, and the plane would almost jump into the air when he let it off.

FLYING IN FORMATION

We read in the news today that, when aircraft get within a mile of each other, it's considered a close encounter. That didn't hold with us. Bombers, of course, flew in formation and were very close together, especially over the target to make a good bomb pattern. But this wasn't the exciting part. With four airfields like ours in about a ten-mile radius and all the squadrons and groups taking off at the same time and jockeying into their respective formation, it was hectic. All the squadrons had different tail markings to help the pilots recognize onto what group to assemble. After a mission, this procedure was done in reverse, with planes peeling out of formation in a prescribed manner. This was complicated, however, since some were by then short of fuel, were badly damaged, or had wounded aboard and wanted precedence to land.

BOMBS AWAY!

The most tense time was over the target. From initial point (IP) to bombs away only took from 5 to 8 minutes, but it seemed like at least 15 or 20 minutes. We, of course, were under the heaviest fire during this period, and the formations tightened up and flew the straight and narrow. The waist gunners would throw out chaff, consisting of a tin foil stuff similar to the tinfoil icicles we used to put on Christmas trees. This chaff was supposed to foul up the enemy radar so they couldn't zero in on your altitude. Presumably, this didn't help your plane but rather the planes coming after you. One time, we had a photographer riding with us; he was throwing out these chaff packages in the prescribed manner of one every two or three seconds. As the flack got heavier, he threw it out faster and faster until finally he just picked up the whole case and threw it out.

After bombs away, the formations just fell apart, spreading out and changing altitude, the theory being that, with a larger area for anti-aircraft gunners to shoot at, the fire would not be so intense. In a few minutes we would be out of fire altogether. During the period of the war I served in, enemy fighter craft were almost gone. The few that were left were well taken care of by American fighter cover. We had both P38s and P51s. It was very comforting to see them all around you.

FLIGHT DETAILS

Our pilot, of course, was the aircraft commander, but he pretty well left everything mechanical to Krawczyk, our engineer. On long missions, when fuel could be a problem, Krawczyk even helped the co-pilot set the throttles on an autolean mixture to conserve fuel. He would also transfer fuel from one engine's tanks to another as they didn't all consume fuel at the same rate. Transferring gas was a ticklish job, and crews sometimes would run an engine out of gas doing it wrong. B24s were somewhat prone to gas leaks in the bomb bay where the Davis wing came clear though the fuselage. For this reason, there was never smoking in the bomb bay. Krawczyk was a sniffer. Whenever he saw fluid, he'd run a finger through it and smell it for identification. After bombs away, he would immediately put on a small, carry-around oxygen bottle— or at 18,000 feet or under, he would quit the O2 altogether—and start checking the plane for damage.

Most of the crew had chest pack parachutes. The pilots had seat packs, which remained in the bucket seats if they walked around the airplane. Mason could not do a long mission without relieving himself. When on oxygen and with mike and headsets to disconnect, plus unbuckling the chute and seat belt, it became a real nuisance. Our ground crew mechanic soldered a funnel to a one-gallon can so Mason could do the job without leaving the controls. He would just reach around and set the can in back of his seat. I rode in the top gun turret just in back of the pilots' seats. The area under my turret is called the flight deck. Entrance to the flight deck was from the bomb bay. The deck was about three feet above the floor of the bomb bay and had both a one-half vertical door and a trap door for an entrance. You could also crawl under this trap door to the nose section of the plane, which is where the navigator, bombardier, and nose gunner rode.

I generally stayed in my turret most of the trip. On the way home one day, Burda got my attention by pulling my leg instead of using the intercom. He pointed at Mason's can, which had been hit with shrapnel and had leaked all over the flight deck. We knew Krawczyk was coming in a few minutes and awaited the reaction. He opened the vertical door and threw the trap door back, which put the flight deck level just below his waist. He saw the fluid, ran his finger through it, and sniffed. "Flack hit the piss can."

The B24 had a longer bomb bay than the B17. To go through it from the waist to the flight deck, there was a narrow catwalk. There were two pillars or braces on either side of the catwalk and attached to the top of the fuselage or the wing going through the plane. These pillars or verticals had the bomb shackles attached to them. These shackles held the bombs and, with some type of electrical solenoid, would release them. There were two sets of these pillars with bomb shackles on them. We generally carried more weight on the front set than the rear as the plane tended to be tail heavy with too much weight on the rear shackles.

We carried various types of bombs, depending on the target and what type of damage was desired. The bombs also varied in weight—from little clusters of incendiaries to large 1,000-pounders. The most common load was 100 pounders, with two to each shackle or 500-pounders one to a shackle. We always flew our own airplane, the "Lady Patricia," and after a few missions, we realized there was always a loud thump that could be felt all over the plane each time bombs were released over the target. We never could figure out what was causing this until the first time we hauled 1,000-pounders.

When bombs away over the target, the bombs were not all released at the same time; with an automatic device, they were released at split second intervals in order to spread the drop over a wider area. When our bombardier released our first load of 1,000-pounders, there was a tremendous thump. When the co-pilot tried to close the bomb bay doors, the open light would not turn off. We were coming off the target by this time so our armourer, Jeff, and Krawczyk investigated. Apparently in the front right bomb bay, the top shackle would always release first, thereby dropping its bomb on the bomb beneath it. This was the source of our thump. With the smaller bombs we had carried in the past, this top bomb would just bounce off its lower neighbor, and all the other shackles would release in proper sequence. With 1,000-pounders however, the top bomb would not clear the one beneath it and was jammed against the side of the bomb bay and the bomb on the lower shackle. We had two 1,000-pounders we had to get rid of before we could land.

Krawczyk had on his parachute harness and a chest pack. The chest pack was about as big as two footballs and weighed about 15 or 20 pounds. It connected to the front of the harness with two snaps. Grabbing a hammer and pry bar, he told me to hang on to him. With Krawczyk's feet on the catwalk, I held the back strap of his chute harness with one hand and the foot rest of my top turret with the other, while he leaned out over the open bomb bay trying to get that bomb loose. He looked over his shoulder at me and made a motion with his head to pull him up. With the engine noise and slipstream noise of the open bomb bay, we had to shout to be heard. Krawczyk unhooked his parachute and tossed it on the flight deck. He told me he couldn't work with that thing hanging in front of him and to not let him drop. Man, I didn't want to drop him, and I was glad he only weighed 130 or 140 pounds.

Back out he went, with his feet on the catwalk and the rest of him with nothing but about 12,000 or 15,000 feet of air between him and the ground. I don't know how long it took or what he did, but finally both bombs dropped at once, and the ship lurched up a little as it always did when the load was lightened. Oh, what a happy day!

I think that everyone that flies or does anything where a little risk is involved feels any bad thing can only happen to someone else. This was my feeling until one mission while on the bomb run I noticed the flack was particularly heavy and seemed to be right at our altitude. Then I remembered not having put on my flack helmet and a piece of flack suit I held over my chest during the run. I unlatched the drop seat of my turret, slid down to the flight deck, and put on my helmet. I had to heave up into the turret in order to pull my seat up into latch position when a chunk of shrapnel hit me just under the eye at the edge of my oxygen mask. It must have pushed my lower lash inside, as it felt like my eyeball was hanging out. However, in a minute or so while batting my eyes, everything came back into focus and felt normal. I announced, "I'm hit in the upper." By that time we were off the target, and Burda, the co-pilot, told me to drop down on the deck, and he'd take a look. There was a little blood, but we both knew it wasn't serious. He took out a handkerchief that had at least 20 missions on it to hold against the wound. I shook my head and pointed at the first aid kit. The pilot was happy. "Wounded aboard. We get to land first." I felt like a fool and tried to talk him out of it but he wasn't having any. It wasn't every day we could land ahead of the pack. The ambulance met us and the whole ball of wax. I decided to relax and enjoy it, with one night in the hospital, nurses, and everything.

After a mission, there was always an interrogation period at group head-quarters. This involved various things like weather, unusual hap-penings, resistance over the target, and such. Crews were questioned as a group, but the officers did most of the talking. The really nice thing about interrogation was the two Red Cross ladies that served coffee and donuts. The coffee and donuts were good, but the best part was seeing two American ladies, especially Fran, who must have been 40 but was pretty.

All of the crews didn't have their own airplane like we did. So any time we didn't draw a mission, some other crew would use the Lady Pat. We didn't like other crews flying our airplane, and most crews didn't like flying strange planes. This was partly due to the fact that each plane was a little different, and also there was mistrust of a ground crew you didn't know. It was on one of our non-flying days we lost our airplane.

A short time ago I received a little book, written in German, which I don't read, with a cover letter written in English. The title of the book is: "1944 1999 La historia dalla curdada dad in bumber B-24J. Die Geschichte eines B-24J-Bomberabstrurzes." The letter was addressed to me but quite obviously written to Gladys Mason, the widow of our deceased pilot, Daryl Mason. I don't know how the writer obtained my address but I have printed the letter in full here.

Freienback, 22, November 1999

Mr Fred Shellenberg
221 S. 10th
Livingstone, MT 59047

Dear Mr. Shellenberg

May I introduce myself first. I had grown up in Chur, Graubunden, Switzerland. In 1944, I was a boy of 11 years. Weekly we had air alert, mostly because the American bomber fleets, which they were on the way from Italy to Germany and visa versa. One of these days it had started the history of "The Lady Patricia," Liberator B-24J. The original 1st pilot of this aircraft was your husband, Daryl R. Mason. I was a eye witness of the tragedy of "The Lady Patricia." With two dead engines the B-24J reached my hometown Chur, where it started to circle. Certainly they started to bail out and a few minutes later we could hear a real bang and we knew that it had crashed down. Last Friday, November 19, 1999, we had held a memorial reunion for "The Lady Patricia." As a historian I'm trying to collect us much as possible memorabilias around this aircraft (in 1944), such as fotos, reports, personal items of the original crew of Mr. Mason. We had picked up the idea to make the story as complete as possible for the descendants to keep alive "The Lady Patricia" story. This brochure was printed just for the 55 years after celebration. If you would like any more information, I'm the most happy to give them to you.

It will be a great pleasure to me, to receive your positive reply.

Very truly yours
Armin Camenisch

So ended the airplane we had picked up in San Francisco and nurtured halfway around the world. I have never heard if any of the crew that was flying her survived. It's probably in my little book, but will have to learn German. [Note: Regarding the loss of the B24 Lady Patricia over Switzerland, I have since learned that the entire crew that was flying her survived.]

After this, we were coming to the end of our missions and, like crews without an assigned plane, had to fly in any bucket of bolts that wasn't being used. With just four or five missions to go, we were flying a brand new plane a crew had just brought over from the States. I remember a mission was over Augsburg... I don't know if that's Germany or Austria, but it was rough. Not being as brave as before I took the little hit, I was much more cognizant that those German gunners were really serious and that they really didn't like us. The anti-aircraft bursts were so close that the plane would bounce around and you could hear the shrapnel hitting the fuselage even over the racket of the engines.

I had my flack helmet on and was hunkered up in that turret, trying to be as small as possible. One isn't supposed to make deals with God, but I said, "Lord, if You'll get us out of this, I will serve You always." And, although I have been the usual backsliding and forgetful Christian, for the most part I have honored that commitment.

We finally came off that target, and good old Krawczyk started sniffing and looking over the airplane. It was a mess. We later counted over 100 holes in it, and the hydraulic systems were completely out. On nearing the base, the landing gear was dropped, and both gears locked. We could check those visually. However, the nose wheel did not lock. Krawczyk and I pushed it out by hand. It would not drop by gravity like the landing gear. There was a little hand system for raising the nose wheel if hydraulics were out, and we cranked it back in and dumped it out again. It still would not lock. This meant that it would collapse back into the fuselage as soon as weight was let down on it. No hydraulics also meant no brakes. The waist gunners buckled parachutes to the 50-caliber gun mounts in the waist windows.

When Mason set her down on the runway, we had the whole show—fire trucks, ambulances, and all. Mason held the nose off the runway as long as possible, and Jeff and Mac dumped the parachutes, which slowed us down, and when the nose started dragging, we came to a rapid stop. The ground crews dragged that nice new airplane off to the junk yard. I'm sure the engines and much other equipment was salvaged.

Flyboys were treated better than ground soldiers. I almost said "real soldiers" but that wouldn't be quite fair. We drew more pay and had more rank. It was a common saying with the Air Corps:

"We're paid for what we do, not for what we know." This also held true in the awarding of medals. Of course, everyone had the European Theatre Operation ribbon, but the ground trooper had to do the Battle of the Bulge or walk from southern France clear to Germany to earn a battle star while we had one for every area of Europe we flew over. Air Medals were automatic for all combat flyers. We got our first one after ten missions and then an oak leaf cluster every five missions after that.

Flight crews also had a rest camp during their tour of duty. Our rest camp was on the Isle of Capri. We had a couple nights in Naples before taking the ferry to Capri. While looking the town of Naples over, we ran into some infantry men also on rest leave. Their camp was at the edge of Naples with squad tents for accommodations. We jokingly asked them if they had nomenclature of the M1 rifle for entertainment. Capri was all it was supposed to be, none of it having been damaged by war. We were entertained and guided all over the island. In the evening two beautiful girls sang to us in Italian, with a supper club atmosphere, and even a short menu to order from. There were two quite sinister-looking civilians on the stage with them, as insurance they would not be rushed by an exuberant bunch of GIs. I never did think we soldiers were music lovers enough to rush those girls.

In the Fifteenth Air Force, all first pilots received a Distinguished Flying Cross during their tour. When Mason was asked what mission he wanted written up for his DFC, he told them he would not take it unless his engineer also got one. He made it stick so Krawczyk was the only enlisted man I personally knew to get one. Colonel Steed sent word down to the squadron for Krawczyk to come up to group for his decoration. It was a mile or two from our squadron area to group, which was housed in a sort of farm villa building, so I walked up with him. There was a WAC officer at the desk outside the Colonel's office. Krawczyk reported in the prescribed manner: "Colonel Steed sent for me."

"What for?" from the WAC.

"He wants to see me."

"What does he want to see you for?"

About this time from inside the Colonel's office, "What's going on out there?"

"There's a Sgt. Krawczyk wants to see you."

Steed walked out of the office and escorted him in. I could hear most of what went on inside. While the colonel pinned the medal on Krawczyk, he stated, "I suppose you will be going into B29s when you get back to the States."

"No, Sir, I'm a B24 man."

This really pressed the colonel's button. He put his arm around Krawczyk's shoulder and said, "You're the kind of men we need in this Air Corps."

This pretty well sums up the crew of the Lady Patricia's tour of duty. We didn't finish all together but one at a time, flying with new crews as needed. Several of the crew left before I did, and not one of them was with me on the ship from Naples to Boston harbor. Four of them I have never seen again, and we were into middle age before the rest of us began to visit back and forth.

Old war, new life.

CHAPTER NINE

THE ALASKA YEARS

Victory in Europe happened while I was home on leave after returning stateside. I was then assigned to garrison duty at Hondo, Texas. This was pretty soft, working a few hours a day in the parachute department of a training base. It's the only place I ever dressed for dinner. Fresh starched suntans every day, and then the difficult decision of whether to eat at the NCO club or mess hall or go to town. During this tough duty, the war ended with Japan.

Uncle Sam had millions of soldiers and sailors to discharge. This was done on a point system. There were points for length of service, service overseas, number of military engagements, and other criteria I can't remember. Many servicemen had many points but were overseas and would not be returned to the states except as a unit. I was already in the states and had more than enough points to qualify for discharge. I was discharged almost in the first batch in 1945.

While I was still at Hondo Air Base in Texas, I somehow learned that the Civil Aeronautics Administration (now the Federal Aeronautics Administration) was hiring radio personnel in Alaska. Still not quite ready to return to small town Livingston, this sounded like a great idea. However, one had to be able to type 40 words per minute to qualify. We had one WAC in the parachute department that could type, and she started teaching me to use the correct fingers.

I took my discharge at Ft. Douglas in Utah, and well heeled with my mustering-out pay, I boarded a bus for Seattle, Washington. On the way I stopped in Olympia, Washington, where the nice lady I had boarded and roomed with while there before enlisting helped me pick out a suit. When being mustered out of the service, each person was given a little gold American Eagle lapel pin. This pin was referred to as "The Ruptured Duck." I attended a USO dance that evening with many soldiers and sailors still in uniform, myself being the only one in civvies and my new lapel pin as proof of service. Having the only ruptured duck in the room that evening, I received more attention from the young lady volunteers than I was used to… even a monkey falls out of a tree once in a while.

On to Seattle where, with my veteran's preference, I qualified for the air traffic radio job except I only typed 10 words per minute. There wasn't another class starting for a month, and I was promised a job if I could demonstrate 40 words per minute at that time. When I reported for the school, they tested me, and I was still short at 32 words per minute. However, these Alaska Air Traffic jobs had been filled by civilians that wanted to come stateside and also many army operators that were eligible for discharge, so I was admitted with the small shortfall.

CAA SCHOOL

At army radio school, we only had to copy Morse code at 10 words per minute with a pencil. With the CAA, we had to copy 30 words per minute with a typewriter. The school consisted of gaining this requirement plus procedure used in air traffic control, voice communications, taking and copying weather reports, and just learning the bureaucratic approach.

One of the instructors at the Seattle school was an ex-Navy radioman. He was instilling in us the need for brevity and concise wording in communications. Using limited wording while still getting the message across made for faster transmission and communication during heavy traffic periods. He gave as an example of perhaps the most perfect message ever transmitted: "Sighted sub, sank same." It's amazing how some little phrase can sometimes solidify an existing philosophy or perhaps begin a new one. Whether this is the origin of my habit of answering most questions with a "yup" or "nope," I don't know, but, this little treatise notwithstanding, I can't think of very many words to describe most situations.

After about six weeks of school, 15 or 20 of us were flown to Alaska. We flew there in "King Chris," a DC3 piloted by a man named Jefford. He was one of the best known pilots in Alaska and the CAA's chief pilot. He did many rescues and probably had the best instrument-equipped plane in service. The DC3 is a Douglas aircraft, known as a C47 in the military. It was a two-engine craft and was extensively used by nearly every airline of that time. There was one stop at Annette Island in southeastern Alaska to fuel and leave some new operators for that area. The rest of us landed in Anchorage, which was where the regional office was located. Everyone was assigned to various locations from there.

Naknek Air Base

Being unmarried, I was assigned to a remote station called Naknek Air Base. The civilian CAA was running the communication for the Army Air Corps. Naknek is a fishing village located on the south side of Bristol Bay, with the airbase being about 12 or 15 miles up the Naknek River. It's on the Alaska Peninsula and is actually the mainland portion before the string of Aleutian Islands. Our station was somewhat of a relay between military and civilian. Most of the flights through our airspace were military flights to the Aleutians servicing the military that were stationed on many of the islands. All of the operators we worked on the chain with were old timers and hot operators. They didn't have much patience with a newcomer. My first day on the job was a nightmare. With only Morse code, called CW for carrier wave, during a heavy traffic time, it was difficult to get on the circuit.

After someone finished their traffic, several stations would try to get the floor, so to speak.

With a whole stack of messages to send, I was waiting for some guy to finish his stack. While waiting, I lit a cigarette, throwing the match in the waste basket. Just then there was an opening, and I grabbed the key and had the circuit. I started sending to the various CW addresses. By then, the waste basket was flaming up beside the shoulder of my sending arm. The station chief noticed and, with a "keep on sending," threw it outdoors. I wasn't about to let go of that key.

Later we had an operator that was new but hot. He could copy as fast as anyone could send. Knowing he was new on the circuit, the hotshots were trying to snow him under. He was copying some guy that was trying to send faster than he was capable of. Dan finally broke in and keyed the CW message, "Send faster, you slob."

After the pecking order was established on circuits, it was really a very friendly place to work, and there was a lot of hamming or chatter when things were slow. Back toward the Alaska mainland, we worked Kodiak Island. It was all civilian operators, most of them having been there most of the war. Many of them were women. When working Kodiak, we would key INT Y L, which means, "Are you a young lady?" If the answer was affirmative, the guys would immediately start romancing.

There was a young man named Dick who had spent the entire war at Naknek and had been romancing one of the YLs at Kodiak for almost that whole period. They, of course, had exchanged letters and photographs during this time and were as well acquainted with each other as anyone could be without having met face to face. The lady was quitting her job and moving back to the States so Dick got a few days off to meet her in Anchorage. The night before Dick was to leave, our Station Chief put on a party. There were the usual refreshments, one of which consisted of one quart of whiskey and one quart of water seasoned with army powdered lemon juice. This concoction was pure dynamite, especially to a guy like Dick, who rarely touched anything. That night he was poured a water glass full of the stuff. Dick quickly became mellow and was anticipating his next day visit. We all started to urge him, "Marry the girl."

"I can't marry her. I've never seen her."

"Dick, you know her personality after writing and working with her for nearly three years. You know she is pretty. Marry her!" Dick procrastinated for some time but finally admitted that he would marry her if she would have him. A couple days later, he came back from Anchorage all smiles. He had bought her a ring, and after a month in the States, she was coming back for the wedding.

We went to work on Dick again: "You can't marry her! You've only seen her for a couple days."

"She's a nice girl, and we're going to get married."

There is a happy ending to this story; they married and, at my last knowledge, had a couple kids and were very happy, proving you can have a successful romance speaking in CW.

The Alaska Peninsula was truly a wild place serviced primarily by transport and passenger planes to the large airstrips and then by bush pilots on skis in the winter and floats in the summer. One time I hopped a ride with a busher to Naknek village during fishing season, which was a mistake. The town was packed with fishermen, and with no place to stay, I had to bed down at the jail. That jail was the dirtiest place I have ever slept in. I could hardly wait to get home for a shower. I knew the Marshall, and he, along with his lone prisoner, welcomed me. The prisoner was in for the duration of fishing season, which is only one month, for getting drunk. With only one month to make your year's living, the law says, there will be no drinking in Naknek during fishing season. At that time, there were no motor boats in the portion of Bristol Bay that Naknek was located in. Only sail boats were in use as the fishing was done with gill nets on the surface of the bay. Sailboats with their centerboards pulled up could go over the nets without tangling.

The next day I headed back to the air base, bumming a ride with a bush pilot that was hauling supplies to a geodetic crew up the river. Naknek had a small lake that served float planes with a little dock at one end. I crawled on top of the freight, and the pilot poured the gas to it... but didn't quite make it. When the throttle is cut, the floats settle into the water, and the plane slows down. He circled back to the dock and threw off one 50-pound sack of flour. With that little bit less weight, he lifted off. He should have thrown me out and really lifted off easily.

Another trip I made was to Dillingham, located on the north side of Bristol Bay and on the mainland of Alaska. It was also a fishing village, but it sported a government-sponsored hospital with one doctor and two nurses. While there, I observed a native man with his wife and a two- or three-year-old child in a long narrow boat, probably 20 feet long with a 5-horse outboard, taking off up the river to a winter trapping cabin. The boat was completely loaded with winter supplies and covered with a tarp. There were five or six sled dogs riding on top of the freight.

Nearly every small cabin or house in the village had a team of sled dogs, each tied to a little dog house. I purchased a spaniel-type dog from a native lady for $5. It was the only dog running loose in the town, causing all the others to bark.

The next day, getting back home was a problem as the cloud ceiling was about 40 or 50 feet. Another man and myself finally talked a pilot into flying us across the bay. There were 8 or 10 planes pulled up on the beach; with the tide out, they were 100 feet or more from the water. Red Flinnsberg, our pilot, fueled his gull wing Stinson with 5-gallon tins of gas. The empty cans were just thrown onto the mud flat in front of the plane. Red started the engine and slid down the mud, running over empty tins with the floats, and into the bay. The bay was absolutely glassy with no wind.

With the plane heavily loaded with freight, two passengers, and my little dog, it would not get up on the step for takeoff. Floats will lift up on top of the water much easier with some waves. Red calmly puffed on a corn cob pipe and methodically pulled back and forth on the stick until we finally lifted off. We flew across the bay at about 25 feet of altitude and then up the Naknek River to the airbase. The clouds were lower than the banks of the river in some places. After dropping us off, I later found out he became a hero for flying a woman that was having trouble in childbirth back to the Dillingham hospital. I believe Red was the only pilot flying that day.

Naknek Air Base had three or four married couples and several bachelors. The married couples had modern government housing. The single men lived in the bachelor officer quarters. There was 1 army officer with 15 or 20 enlisted men left in 1946. There were warehouses, many with supplies, gasoline dumps, and barracks all around the runways. Most of this was abandoned; however, the remaining army personnel were presumably the caretakers. There were jeeps we could use with 50-gallon drums of gasoline by the hundred to fuel them. During the winter, when the tundra was frozen, the jeeps were put to use to go to the village or upriver to fish for sea-run rainbow. The army also had boats and outboards we could use. The only entertainment was to hunt, fish, or trap. I worked the midnight-to-eight shift and engaged in these pastimes nearly every day.

COLD STORAGE EGGS

Getting off shift at eight in the morning made me late for breakfast at the army mess hall. Connie, the cook was a civilian, and quite independent with either the army or other civilians he dealt with. After preparing a late meal for me once or twice, I was told to fry my own eggs. I cracked the first one on the hot griddle, and it was nearly a foot in diameter. I scraped it into the waste. The next egg was the same, and I started getting rid of it. Connie said, "What's going on?" I told him the eggs didn't seem very fresh to me, and I was looking for some good ones. Connie informed me that those eggs had only been in cold storage for a couple years and were perfectly good. He further informed me that cold storage eggs, if turned once a week, would last practically forever. A true Alaskan didn't like fresh eggs. There was no flavor to them.

TANANA

After about a year, I had the chance to transfer to Tanana, a small village located where the Tanana and Yukon Rivers come together. This was a much smaller station with more emphasis on weather observations than air traffic. My stay in Tanana was only three months in the dead of winter. This was the winter of 1946-47 when record cold temperatures were recorded. Snag in Yukon Territory made a record low of 82 degrees below zero, with Tanana having 70 below for several days, and nearly half the time I was there, it was 50 below. My first day there, I walked to the village with a pair of butyl rubber shoe packs. I walked into the Northern Commercial Co. store and kicked the stove to warm my feet. That rubber was so hard it sounded like a sledge hammer. The Northern Commercial manager advised me to buy some mukluks, which I did; they are soft and much warmer. He also asked to buy any paper dollars or pennies I had. He sent the dollars to Fairbanks and threw the pennies into the river. He felt it was one of his duties to keep the town free of this degrading currency. In this type of cold, air traffic almost came to a stop because one plane taking off or landing socked in the air strip. It was absolutely wind still, and the vapor of one plane could take two or three days to drift off the strip. The Aurora Borealis, or Northern Lights, were fantastic in this cold clear environment.

OLD SOURDOUGHS

Except for the CAA personnel and one doctor and one nurse, nearly everyone else was native—either Eskimo or Indian. There were also three or four men left over from the Alaskan gold rush in the late 1800s. These men had come up for the gold and never returned to the States. Some of them married and had families. One of these was named Starr. He had walked from the lower 48 to Alaska through Canada. Another of these old sourdoughs lived across the runway from the CAA housing. I spent lots of time with him, listening to stories of the gold rush days. The miners would carry their gold dust poke loose in their pockets. When showing it off in a saloon, it would dribble on the floor. After some of these tales, I finally got around to asking if he ever made a good strike. Well, he had, about $25,000 in one summer. I asked what he did with his poke. He got rid of it just like those other dumb guys. Then I asked how he made a living all the years since the gold rush. "I was a contractor on the Alaska Railroad at one time."

"The heck you were." I envisioned heavy equipment and hired crews.

"I had a wheelbarrow and hauled dirt by the yard."

Nearly everyone in the village, including the old prospectors, had three kinds of income. They cut cord wood for the river steamer; they dried salmon, which was baled and sold to Northern Commercial; and they trapped in the winter. In addition, the mining men continued to stake claims and prospect with the idea of luring some investor to put in a dredge or some other means of mining. Other than the government employees, I would say the average family income in Tanana was under $500 per year. Transportation was by dog team or bush pilot, and there were young people in their twenties who had never been to Fairbanks, only about an hour's flight time away.

Probably the leading citizen of Tanana was "Old Man" Thompson, a holdover from the gold rush days. I never knew his first name. He was the postmaster and the commissioner. The commissioner was appointed and the only real law in Tanana. This was sort of like being mayor, police chief, and county attorney all in one. Once, when picking up my mail, I noticed a bedroll and an old rifle in the corner. I asked him who it belonged to. "It belongs to so and so. I have him in the back room, thawing him out so we can bury him in the spring. He froze to death trying to get to town after his cabin burned down."

"Why thaw him out?" I asked. He was in quite a contorted position apparently, and Thompson felt he would store better horizontally.

"What's going to happen to the rifle and bedroll."

"They belong to the territory," from Thompson.

"What's the territory going to do with them?"

"Sell them."

I asked the crucial question: "How much does the territory want for the rifle?"

"Five bucks."

"I'll just take that sucker." It was a nice old 1876 Winchester, 45-60 caliber. I still have it, my favorite souvenir of Alaska.

SLED DOG RACES & CARNIVALS

Even the small villages observed some type of celebration, and what could be more appropriate than a winter carnival for Tanana, Alaska? The festivities centered around a sled dog race with a dance in the old Army Hall that night. Other than the stores, the Army Hall was the largest building in Tanana. It was a left-over from when the army was stationed there in the early 1900s. I wasn't enough of a historian to find out why the army was there, but there were still old photographs of army groups and officers hanging on the walls of the building.

At that time, the world's champion sled dog racer lived in Tanana. This was before the millionaires began competing in the Iditarod. I do not recall his name, but he was a very progressive Eskimo man with a fine family. He had a handmade racing sled, and his husky dogs were of the smaller variety. Most men of the town had a racing sled; 4 or 5 feet long, it was used for racing or quick trips to town. They all owned work sleds, too, 10 or 12 feet long and used to haul supplies and family to remote areas for extended periods of trapping. As I recall, when temperatures were in the 50 degrees below area, nearly all dog work ceased, as the cold would frost their lungs.

Carnival day dawned bright and sunny, with modest temperatures in the zero range. The race was held on the Tanana river ice with a starting line near the village; then it was around an island a mile or two downriver and back to the starting point. The river, of course, was frozen with 25- or 30-foot banks up to the level of the village. The banks were quite steep with only occasional places one could come off them to river level. The men with their racing sleds and teams—varying from 6 to 10 dogs, all of them yipping and barking and prone to fight another team in their proximity—started to assemble near the starting line on the river ice. I think every 1 of the 200 or 300 residents were on the ice and in a very festive mood. Then over the bank came a young unmarried man, somewhere in his early 20s. Obviously the idol of all the young girls, he had a strong work team of barking dogs and a big heavy sled at least 12 feet long. The crowd cheered one of their favorite sons as he, with a big smile, modestly accepted their adulation and slid into his place on the starting line.

The starting gun was sounded, and the dozen or so racers took off. The men stood on the back of the sled runners and pushed with one leg to help the dogs up to speed. Needless to say, the young guy with the heavy work sled didn't make a jackrabbit start, but eventually he was speeding across the ice… until he pulled even with his home about 200 yards toward the island. When his dogs reached that point, they started straight up the river bank, heading for home. He was yelling "Whoa! Whoa!" and putting his entire weight on the drag brake sleds are equipped with. Nothing could keep that big team from going home. The crowd went absolutely wild. No crowd of athletic fans ever greeted an unexpected happening with more enthusiasm or appreciation.

FAIRBANKS

Next came Fairbanks, the largest city of the Alaska inland. In Fairbanks was located the north end of the Alaska Railroad and a air transportation center to the Seward Peninsula, across the Arctic Circle to Point Barrow and to scattered settlements to the east before entering Canada's Yukon Territory. Fairbanks also had the

Alaska University, a country club, and a daily newspaper. Air traffic was heavy at our CAA station, working both civilian and military aircraft, and we also disseminated weather data from ships at sea, all of Alaska and Thule, Greenland to Canada and the US, and then we reversed the situation by sending U.S. and Canadian weather to the outer reaches of Alaska. The teletype room consisted of about 10 machines that, during three hourly and six hourly intervals, we were busy receiving, taping, and retransmitting. It was hectic but rather fun, with tapes crisscrossing the room and reams of weather reports to be sent to the Fairbanks weather bureau.

FLYING COUNTRY

This was flying country, with dozens and maybe hundreds of bush pilots. They were characters with many stories and planes. They were, to Alaska, what I imagine the old time cowboy and his horses were to our West. One of the famous families of Fairbanks were the Weins. I think there was a father with four brothers originally. They had many ups and downs with one of the uppers being Wein Alaska Airlines. I don't recall all the history on them, but several died in crashes over the years, and they were in on many exciting trips and rescues.

I recall one old timer—Archie Ferguson, I believe, was his name. When he flew a cheechauko (tourist, dude, or whatever) over the Arctic Circle, he would cut the engine for a few seconds, telling them there wasn't enough air for fuel combustion. He was also noted for flying with one wing lower than the other, explaining the plane seemed to trim up and fly better that way.

Another pilot that lived a few doors from me was noted for flying while intoxicated. He didn't tell me these stories, but those in the flying circles knew them and swore they are true. After delivering a passenger to Kotzebue, he had a few drinks before returning to Fairbanks. Having a little difficulty with his vision, he asked his buddies, "Just push the tail around and line me up with the runway." After they complied with his request, he poured the coal to it and headed for Fairbanks. Another tale is that he, his wife, and a friend were imbibing during flight. He and his wife were having a fight, and she became so upset that she pushed the door open and jumped out. The friend grabbed her and held her by a leg or arm, don't know which, but could not pull her back into the plane. The pilot found a cornice of soft drifted snow, slowed the plane down as much as possible, and banking away from the snowdrift, yelled, "Let her drop!" Then he landed the ski-equipped plane nearby, helped his uninjured mate out of the deep snow, and finished the trip.

FLYING LESSONS

During my year at Fairbanks, a veteran friend and I decided it was foolish to waste our GI Bill on a college education so instead we used a chunk of it for flight training and a pilot's license. We trained in Taylorcrafts (T/crafts), Aronicas, and Pipers. This was during the long summer days that only those northern latitudes could give. I did get my license and really enjoyed the flying, but after three separate hair-raising experiences, I decided my mother was right about my inadequacies in regards to keeping my mind on the business. The first was my first solo, cross-country flight from Fairbanks to Big Delta. It was beautiful day, and I was sort of waving my wings back and forth in a falling leaf effect and looking at the blue sky. I happened to look at my watch; an hour had elapsed, and it was now my estimated time to Big Delta. I looked over my shoulder, and there was Big Delta; I had nearly passed it by.

My next flight was with a friend, each of us in our own planes. We were having fun, flying formation some and then peeling off to sashay over the river. Our destination was Nenana, an hour's flight down the river from Fairbanks. We found the town and air-strip fine. We both dragged the airport, looking for the windsock to determine which way to land. I could not spot the wind sock so entered the pattern and set her down. The minute I got on the ground I knew something was haywire because the plane was go-ing much too fast and I couldn't set the tail down. We had landed downwind with about a 20 or 25 mph wind. As an addition to this story, the planes we learned in had no radio equipment, either transmitter or receiver, or we would have used airport facilities for landing instruction. All of our flying was VFR (visual flight rules) with no radio contact.

My last and dumbest flight was a cross-country to Anchorage, a much longer flight. It was again with my Nenana flight friend—

can't remember his name. The trip to Anchorage was uneventful, but the weather forecast for the return to Fairbanks showed some clouds moving in. We both worked the midnight to eight shift and felt we had to get back. The route was through a valley with sizable mountains on both sides. We were under the overcast but, looking ahead, it seemed lower and lower. Not wanting to get into the clouds, I turned back a few miles and climbed on top, planning to drop back down after clearing the mountains. The mountain peaks were sticking out of the clouds so it was easy to navigate and pretty well know our position. After the proper elapsed time, I knew Fairbanks was near. It was just beginning to get dark, and the clouds were showing a few breaks. We were flying close together when we saw lights through a break in the clouds. Fairbanks, what a welcome sight. I slipped through the opening, practically over the field, entered the pattern, and set down. I flew a few times after that, but I had lost much of my enthusiasm.

Road Trip Home

I purchased a car in Fairbanks, and after a fun summer, it was turning winter again. I bid a job in Homer, Alaska, on the Kenai Peninsula—lots of peninsulas in Alaska! I took a month's annual leave and decided to drive the Alcan Highway to Montana, leave my car at home, and fly back to Homer. It was well into winter, and I had learned that a car had to be started every four hours or it would not start without extra effort. When I slept at night, I would always have a friend start my car at least every four hours. Before leaving, I met a man that wanted to go stateside to share expenses with.

It was in the 50 below zero range when we left, and by trading off, we drove for about 24 hours, reaching Whitehorse in Yukon Territory, Canada, about seven in the morning. We stopped at the Whitehorse Hotel. The hotel was full, but the clerk felt there should be a vacancy in an hour or two. We were told to relax in the small lobby and she would wake us when someone checked out. She told me there was a garage a block down the street that would pull my car in to start it when I was ready to leave. I parked my car across the street from the garage and covered it with a blanket. We must have slept a couple hours in the lobby when I checked again with the clerk. Still no vacancy. It was very cold, and I told my partner, "Let's go try that car." It started right up so down the road we went.

There were roadhouses every hundred miles or so. These consisted of just a few buildings that furnished gas, food, and in most cases some kind of lodging. My car was a two-door sedan. The heater just would not warm the inside up, so in addition to being warmly dressed, we had a blanket to cover up with. We stopped at many of the roadhouses for gas or meals or just a break in the monotony. At one of the places we stopped for breakfast, we visited with the waitress, and she asked for a ride to Calgary or somewhere south. We told her it would be cold, even in the front seat between us, but, if she still wanted to go, to get ready. Then she advised us that her husband also wanted to go. While they were gone, the cook told us her husband was very jealous and to be very careful around the wife. We discussed this situation and decided that probably having a guy's wife between us under a blanket in the front seat was not conducive to a friendly relationship with a jealous husband. We bolted our food and took off without them, not a very nice thing to do but a bit more prudent perhaps.

I only recall sleeping in a bed one night on the five-day trip. We stopped at a roadhouse about midnight. There was still a light on. We gassed up, and the man's wife fixed us a meal. They had sleeping facilities, but we voiced our concern about starting the car and not wanting to idle it all night long. The man assured us he would start it during the night and asked if I needed an oil change? The only facility he had for changing oil was an outdoor elevated rack high enough so he could get under the car. "With 40 below zero, you don't want to crawl under that car."

The guy told me, if I wanted a oil change, he would be glad to do it. I think business was rather slow at that roadhouse. He serviced my car, we had a very pleasant night, the lady fixed a good breakfast, and we headed down the road in a warmed-up auto. I have thought of their hospitality since that trip and hoped that their business improved over the years.

The gravel roads were snow-packed for the entire trip, but not slippery. With the cold temperature, it was almost like driving on pavement. The roads were much smoother in winter than they were in summer with the washboarding of a gravel road. It was still winter in Montana but not as much so. I dropped my passenger off in Great Falls and headed on to Livingston, via Helena.

I don't remember but I must have slept for hours after getting home. Park County was changing, my friends were adults, and some of them married. Time waits for no man.

HOMER

Homer, Alaska, was my favorite of the places I lived at and visited in the north country. Alaska was still a territory, and residents could not vote in a presidential election. But there were veterans moving in, and some of them homesteaded under the same Homestead Act of the late 1800s and early 1900s. There was logging, fishing, and of course government work. The Fish and Game, among other agencies, was enlarging. The highway from Homer, on the end of the peninsula to Anchorage, was being started on both ends. The Alaska Road Commission was a large employer, and many of the single guys that were homesteading used that summer employment for their cash crop. CAA employees had government housing near the airport, which houses were by far the best homes in the area. The Rural Electric Coop was just moving into town, generating their power with Cat diesels. Many people didn't yet have electricity or plumbing in that progressive town. The CAA had its own power station with three big diesels for power. The airport was serviced by two airlines on a daily basis. Pacific Northern and Alaska Airlines both stopped in Homer and then continued to Kodiak Island or down the Alaska Peninsula. In addition to a modern lighted runway, there was a small reservoir between the town and the airport that served float planes in summer and skis in winter.

PUT

There was only one resident bush pilot in Homer. His name was Putnam, but everyone called him "Put." Put wanted me to buy his Piper Super Cub and take over his business. When I told him I just barely had a private license, let alone a commercial one, his answer was, "That's how I got started. After a few hours, then you take the commercial test."

Hunting and fishing were the main entertainments of the area, and Put played on my weakness. I had it in mind to bag an Alaska Brown Bear, which is actually an oversize grizzly. All winter long, Put assailed me with bear stories, where to get them and when the hide was prime. Spring was the time to get them, when they first came out of the den. Their fur was at its finest and longest, and they were not shedding until later in the spring. He told me many bear hibernated at Caribou Lake. They didn't really have dens but went into the dense brush on the hill on the east side of the lake. The snow would drift over the brush, giving the bear a snug snow cave to winter in. His advice was to be on top of the hill and, as the bears came out of their winter beds, to pick one out and plug it. Put promised to let me know when the time was right for the coming out. One morning Put came into the station as I was getting off shift at eight in the morning. "Well," he said, "this is the day those bear are coming out of hibernation."

"Good, fly me out to Caribou to the top of that hill."

"Can't do it," Put says. "I have a charter to Seldovia today."

"Put me down for tomorrow, Put."

"It will be too late tomorrow."

"One day can't make that much difference, for crying out loud."

Put explained that this was the day as it had been cloudy and was sunny. This was the very day, he insisted, and by tomorrow, they would be pretty well dispersed. "I'll bet you could get Harry Hegdahl to fly you up there."

"What if the bear don't come out when I get there?"

"When you're on top of that hill, if you don't see a bear, yell, and they will start poking their heads out all over the place."

I caught a ride to town, found Harry, told him my problem, and talked him into flying me up there. Harry was a very pleasant guy with a wife and kids. He worked for the Alaska Road Commission in summer and ran a small movie theater in winter. He had just advertised the movie, "State Fair," which was a very recent release. Everyone went to it, but it turned out to be "State Fair" with Will Rogers, released in the early thirties. I think Harry was as surprised as his customers.

Shortly, we took off in Harry's two-place ski-equipped plane. We landed on top of the hill overlooking Caribou Lake and crawled out into about a foot and half of snow. I started walking to the edge of the hill, looked back at Harry, and asked, "Where is your rifle?"

"You didn't say anything about bringing a rifle."

"Cripes, Harry, this is dangerous game." We both walked to

the crest of the hill and looked over. It was just like Put had described. The hillside was quite obviously drifted deep with snow with some brush sticking out here and there. We searched the hillside but could see nothing that would indicate a bear had made a opening. I remembered Put's instruction to give a yell to disturb their winter sleep.

"Hey!" it came out almost a squeak, my rifle at ready. Even Harry looked a little nervous.

"Yo!" a little louder. I was in a half crouch, safety off. Nothing moved.

Pretty soon I was bellering like a bull, with an occasional, "Yahoo!" from Harry. The hill was absolutely quiet, not a track showing. As I began to get warm, my fertile brain started going over the sequence of events, and I eventually arrived at the conclusion that Put had spent the last three months setting me up for this fiasco. And now, in retrospect, I believe Harry also was in on the whole deal.

The next morning, Put was again at the station about shift change. "How was the hunt?"

"There wasn't much going on up there."

"Maybe it was a little early. Shall we try it again today?"

"No thanks, Put. I didn't really want to shoot a bear anyway."

And I never did buy his airline either!

A New Vocation

After a year at Homer I decided no more of that easy government money. The Alaska Road Commission superintendant agreed to give me a summer job. I quit the CAA after New Year's 1949. First, I flew home and ate some of my mother's good cooking. My brother Art and I put in some wheat in April, and I went back to Homer about the first of May. It was still winter up there, and I lived with friends for nearly a month.

My first job with the road commission was putting in a new dock, the old one having been destroyed during a winter storm. It was rather spooky working about 90 feet above the water. The tides in that area are enormous, especially in the spring and fall. After a month on the dock, I moved to a construction camp about five miles from Homer and became a truck driver. It was fun work, and I was back to living in a tent like army days.

One of the men in my tent was the engineer of the job. He was a jolly guy and took a little ribbing about the easy job. One day I commented to him, "Why do you keep peeking through that spy glass? I could lay out a better road than this with my naked eye."

"You just don't understand road building."

"What's to understand?"

"First, we build them, then we pave them, and then we straighten them!"

I was still working for the government, but not for long. That fall, when the rains came, construction ceased. It was back to Park County for good.

CHAPTER TEN

ON MY OWN

No job, minimal savings, and worst of all, no real plan... I was, as the Alaska bush pilots would say, "Flying by the seat of my pants." My brother Art had teamed up with Ben Strickland in a custom hay baling venture. They both attended college in the winter, and in the summer they baled hay for ranchers and farmers tired of fighting loose hay in windy country. Ben and Art bought one of the first two self-tying balers in Park County. It was New Holland string tie with a Wisconsin air-cooled engine to power the baler itself. Instead of using a tractor for towing, they used a jeep. The jeep had plenty of power for pulling, and it gave them the advantage of being able to go much easier when the hay windrow was light and of being able to achieve a much faster road speed when moving from one job to another. Ben was about ready to finish college, so I bought out his share.

The winter of 1949 was rough with lots of snow. With a

farmhand hay fork on the front of a tractor and with our baler, we baled many tons out of loose haystacks. The bales were then trucked into eastern Montana and North Dakota. Art and I started buying milk cows that winter, and we also brought my mother's little farm up to the requirements for selling grade A milk—milk sold in the bottle for consumption; the lower grades were used for ice cream and cheese.

We started selling our milk to the Yellowstone Dairy, which had just been purchased by Bill and John Anderson. They installed a modern pasteurizing and ice cream plant in the Miles block on South Second Street. They were comparatively new in the business and were still learning the ins and outs. One day Bill was walking down the alley between Main and Second Streets when he ran into Carl Wilcoxsin. Carl's ice cream plant was across the alley from the Yellowstone Dairy plant. Wilcoxsin's was a premium ice cream of many years' standing. Much of it was marketed in Yellowstone Park, as well as at Wilcoxsin's soda fountain and confectionary. Carl told Bill, "Come into my plant. I want to show you some things about making ice cream."

Bill said, "Why would you want to do that? We're competitors."

Carl's answer was: "If we don't improve the quality of your ice cream, you will destroy the entire industry."

So goes business in Livingston, Montana.

Art and I were having problems, also. We didn't know a good milk cow from a poor one, but were learning fast. If they didn't produce much milk, they were a poor cow. We then started buying cows that had been tested on their production—by DHIA testing (Dairy Herd Improvement Association). The testing was accomplished by a licensed tester coming to your farm once a month, weighing both morning and evening milk, and testing each cow for percent of butterfat in the milk. After a year, this gave a close approximation of the cow's production for the entire year.

We also began purchasing registered Holsteins with proven production. We purchased one cow at the Winter Fair in Bozeman for $700. I believe this was the highest price paid for a milk cow in Montana up to that time. Her name was "Bridger Lee Friend Paul" and of the breeding by Lawrence Christie at his Bridger Dairy farm. We only milked for two more years and then auctioned off our herd. This particular cow went back to the Gallatin Valley and became the highest life time producer in the Gallatin Valley.

It was during my cow milking period that I met a lovely young lady, Viola Evans, who was teaching physical education at the high school. I met her through an old friend of my mother's, Bernice Fuher. Bernice's husband Bill managed Miles' Dry Goods and later had a women's wear store of his own. Bernice and Bill had a large home on West Park Street and usually had two teachers rooming with them. Miss Buck, a long time English teacher at the high school, contacted Vi after she had signed on to teach and suggested she take a vacant room. Bernice's acquaintance with my mom was from the homestead days in Sweetgrass County. My mother babysat Bernice as a small child. Bernice was quite short and slightly rotund, which she accepted quite philosophically. She would hold a small bonbon up and, viewing it, would say: "This little thing couldn't possibly weigh more than an ounce or two, so I couldn't gain more than that amount eating it. And what's an ounce or two to a person like me?"

Bernice also had another weakness. She always said only nice things about people. She suggested me to Vi, telling her I had been in Alaska and was quite well off financially after my three years up there. This, of course, proves that people that only say nice things have it wrong about half the time. As Bill Strong once stated, "Some of the smartest and best things I ever did were pure accidents." This holds true for me also, especially after Vi agreed to marry me.

During our courtship, of course, I introduced her to friends and family. One of the first introductions was to my old friends, Bill and Mary Strong. They had three kids by this time, and during our visit Bill had to correct them. "Cheryl, get out of there. Penny, cut that out. And you, what's your name, will you stop that?" Vi got a large charge out of that until she came to a family dinner where she met Wes Strong, who was married to my sister Evelyn, and the rest of my immediate family. It was a Sunday dinner, after which the conversation centered around the doings of various acquaintances. These people were referred to as "the thing down at the corner," or "what's his name up the creek," or "the guy with the banged-up red pickup." After leaving this enlightening company, Vi wondered if we ever called people by name as, during a whole afternoon, there were only a few names mentioned. Fortunately, Vi finally figured out who what's his name was and could carry on an intelligent conversation with the best of us.

Vi and I were married, the tenth of June, 1951, in Polson, Montana. She was born in Polson so, between us, we claimed two of the nicer areas in the state. The day before going to my wedding, I went downtown and bought a new suit. I must have had trouble finding one to fit. When I took the coat off after the wedding, Vi said the pants were gathered toward the back and looked like elastic under the belt. I have always had help purchasing clothes since then. We toured two nations on our four-day honeymoon, Canada and Montana. I borrowed my mother's car for this trip as, with my natural good taste, I felt a Jeep without doors would not be appropriate.

Making the change from farming as a bachelor to farming married was an easy transition. Vi was a good cook, just like my mother. Art started easing out of our casual partnership, taking an apprentice lineman job with Montana Power. As I write this, I am wondering if Art ever took anything out of the farming business when we split up. I will have to ask him.

After disbursing our small dairy herd, I started buying calves at the Bozeman Auction Yard and running them to yearlings. I continued to custom bale hay and did whatever else came along, including two winters working in the Northern Pacific RR roundhouse. About this time, the Lane family of Three Forks, Montana, started a large cattle-feeding operation on the west edge of their town. They took cattle and finished them with grain, charging so much a pound on the gain. This looked like an effortless way to make money. My wife had saved about $1,500 during her teaching career with the idea of buying a new car. Who needs a new car with a Jeep to ride around in? She very sweetly surrendered the whole amount, and with what I could scrape up, we bought 12 or 14 yearling steers to put on feed.

I had bought quite a few weaned calves, mostly odds and ends but never high quality stuff to put on feed. I was sitting at the auction next to a guy that seemed in the know and told him my plan. Six or eight nice steers came through, and I started bidding on them. The friendly stranger I was sitting by nudged me and said, "Tell them to turn that red-necked one back." I did this, purchasing the remaining ones. Then they auctioned off the cut back, which I purchased for a few cents less per pound. Wow, I was learning the cattle business… what fun! I had my day's purchases trucked to the Three Forks feedlot.

In about three months, my steers were finishing off, but the market was down. A buyer from Idaho called me with an offer on the steers right at the lot. I turned him down and, instead, trucked them to the Billings Auction Yards. They sold for even less than the Idaho buyer had offered me, and I had the trucker to pay for. Now the cattle business wasn't quite as much fun… I have found through a long and happy life that I am a better buyer than seller. When I want to buy something, I have to have it right now, but sometimes things can't be sold that rapidly.

HENRY

In later years, I became acquainted with a well-known cattle buyer named Henry who moved in next door to me. He came to Montana in the 1920s and was a sheep buyer to begin with. He purchased sheep from many big producers, including Charles Bair of the Two Dot-Martinsdale area. As sheep raising decreased in Montana, Henry started buying cattle. Henry was unique in that he purchased cattle and resold them, rather than just order buying on someone else's account. Henry had an expression, "When you own the cow, she's worth more." One doesn't buy something unless they feel it's worth at least slightly more than the person is selling it for.

For years Henry lived in the Bozeman Hotel. This gave him a free answering service when he was on the road. Henry also fed cattle on his own account in Iowa. He would sometimes take a trip to the feedlot to see how his stock was doing. On one occasion, he decided to team up with another buyer, Lenox Badger. Badger also had cattle on feed near Henry's. Both of them were getting to an age that driving was a chore, so they hired Brad Palmer, a younger version of these cattle traders, to do the driving. The agreement was that Henry would buy the meals, and Lenox would furnish the gas. Brad, driving in the 85- to 90-mile-per-hour range, got them into Rapid City, South Dakota, too early for lunch. Henry bought an ice cream cone there, with the next stop being at the hotel near the feeding operation. This really raised Henry's dealing instincts, having his old friend pay all the gas while he only had to pop for three ice cream cones.

CHILDREN

A year after our marriage, the first of our three kids was born on April 26, 1952. It was a boy, and we named him Tom. He was big, and he was happy. By the time, Tom was three, I had him driving the jeep. I picked up hay bales out of the field with a trailer, putting the Jeep into low, low gear and telling Tom all he had to do was drive between the bales. He knelt on the front seat, loving the work and smiling from ear to ear, but somehow he missed seeing a lot of bales. He was looking at me for approval instead of where he was driving. We both had lots of fun working together.

Vi Shellenberg with son Tom in 1953.

*The series of photos on these two pages shows the different
stages of the Park County High School.*

The photo above shows the original building.

*The top photo on facing page shows how the contractors incorporated
the original building into an updated building.*

*The bottom photo on facing page shows how the WPA in 1938-1939
took the building and totally changed its look*

High School, Livingston, Montana.

Park County High School

CHAPTER ELEVEN

GOING INTO BUSINESS

A fter a few years of farming, even I could see I was getting nowhere fast. I had priced land with the idea of expanding, but even in those long ago days of lower land prices, it was hard to pencil out how to pay for it with profits. About this time, we had Tom's baby pictures taken, which showed me how easy it was to take good pictures of a good-looking boy. My wife and I talked over the idea of opening a photo studio. Never having difficulty making a decision, I was enrolled in a correspondence course almost immediately.

CHRIS

I also asked Chris Schlechten, a Bozeman photographer, for advice and help. He obliged by letting me do his dark room work for one winter. The pay was nil, but the company was good, and I learned under a man I consider the best photographer the state ever produced. Chris was not only a good photographer but he also had most of the attributes of a true artist. One of these was his ability to be about six months behind on his orders. However, the results were so good people put up with him.

This is ancient history, but Chris and a man named Racine put out a very famous and very rare annual for Montana State College sometime in the late 20s or early 30s. The photography was done by Chris while Racine was the business manager. The photos of all the school groups were taken in the usual manner. However, Chris photographed a hobo, sometimes referred to as a "knight of the road," in many different positions. Then he dubbed the hobo into nearly all the groups. He might be lying down in front of the group, or you might just see his head peeking over the top, or around the side of the glee club or the cheer leaders or whatever. The basketball team was composed with ten Butterfinger candy bars. The names of the players were, of course, dutifully listed under the photo. The annual was printed without word ever leaking out, but after only a very few were delivered, the powers that be saw one. Sales were stopped immediately, and the bulk of them were destroyed. Where is the ACLU when you need it?

Chris was a great instructor and a good friend. We were also in the National Guard together in the 1950s. He was in the band while I was in a tank company. He was photographing tank crews, using flash to fill the dark shadows of bright sunlight. One of my crew asked him why he used flash on a bright day. Chris answered, "I don't trust the sun."

SHELLENBERG STUDIO

To round out preparations for opening a photo studio, I purchased a house at 515 West Park Street. I borrowed $8,500 from my mother to pay for it. Interestingly, I was the second owner of this house. I purchased it from a Mrs. Turner whose husband had been an engineer on the railroad. It had been built in 1900, and the abstract showed that the Northern Pacific RR had owned the land previously. With very little effort, the house lent itself to making a well laid out studio, with camera room, darkroom, sales room, and all.

We also purchased a Ford car with roll-up windows and upholstery. A Jeep without doors would not do for an up and coming business man. The Jeep was about all that was left of the partnership my brother Art and I had. One cold winter day, I bundled my only boy up real warm, put him on the front seat of that jeep, no seat belt, and headed for Helena where Art and his new wife were living. I told Art, "I've used up my half of this Jeep. The rest of it is yours." Art is the fixer of the family. In a short time, that Jeep had doors, the dents were gone, it was repainted, and I almost asked for my half back. Art sold that vehicle a few years later and got more for it than we had paid in 1949. Inflation was rearing its ugly head. But inflation is good for people in debt. You're paying off with dollars that are not worth as much and easier come by than when things are tight.

Shellenberg Studio opened for business January 1, 1953. People were nice to me and very understanding. I had to retake my first baby three times. I had taken my big old 5x7 view camera apart and reassembled it wrong. I'm glad not to be a doctor as you don't get three chances to learn on. With all my bumbling and learning, things progressed slowly, very slowly. After a couple years, we got an Eastman Kodak dealership, which led to selling film and cameras. We had the first copy machine in Livingston. It was a Kodak product, called a Verfax, and made a wet copy that was squeegeed off and dried in the machine. In a few years, dry copiers took over, but we made a lot of customers through our copying.

The house I had converted into a studio was 40 feet from the sidewalk. I felt that getting out to the street would give me more room and attract more notice. I contracted with a local contractor to build this addition. During construction, a salesman for Pako photofinishing products called on me. I told him there was a Red Cross blood drawing downtown and that I wanted to get in before the railroaders that came after four o'clock. He said, "I'll just go down and give a pint with you." While we were being bled, I purchased a black and white roll film processing plant from him. The printer was the latest electronic type, analyzing a negative and giving proper exposure automatically. I approached my brother John to be the darkroom man while I did the camera work, retouching, and sales. We started doing film processing for drug stores and also developed a mail order business. Things were coming together, and even my banker quit hiding when I came in the door.

Christmas Card 1960. L to R: Susan, Tom, & Kathy.

During these busy times, Vi presented our family of three with daughter Susan on August 7, 1954, and on June 6, 1958, with another daughter, Kathy. The five of us also acquired a house, after having lived over the store or in my mother's old farm house, most of our married lives. A normal work week at the store was 60 hours, but it was a rare day we did not have our evening meal together. Having a store was ideal for our kids also. They never had an allowance but had a job, starting at about first grade. These jobs consisted of hauling waste paper and boxes to the alley, sweeping, dusting, and drying and sorting prints for the photofinishing. Kathy was so small she could barely reach a table to fold mailers for the mail orders. She would crease them with her elbow. My brother John also added to the confusion with nick names and various other forms of teasing. He called Susan, Weird Harold. When he needed something, he would yell, "Weird!" and Sue would come running. If I do say so myself, my kids not only learned to work but also to work fast and to work accurately. Perhaps my own father had something to do with this. When he asked a kid to get the hammer, this didn't mean shuffling off; it meant on the double.

ART GALLERY

My new store front was quite attractive. Fred Martin—editor of the *Park County News,* a weekly paper—gave us some good write up, and we also started doing some press photography for him. But I could not fill up that nice new 25x40 foot store with cameras. Through our church, Vi and I become friends with Vernon and Helen Stanley. He was head of Human Resources in Livingston, but his true love was art. He was not only a student of art, but also an appreciator and even practiced various styles of painting himself. The first painting I ever bought was from Vernon, and I still have it. We started hanging a few paintings to sell for him and for a friend of his. Then we became acquainted with Dick and Dorothy Murphy. They were absolute enthusiasts about art and painting. The first thing you know, we had to change the name from Shellenberg Studio to Shellenberg Studio Gallery.

Snook's Art Shop in Billings was mostly an art supply store, but it also sold paintings. Harold Ruth of Billings opened the Brown Barn Gallery on the heights the year after we opened. There was only one gallery in Jackson Hole, Wyoming, the Trailside Gallery, owned by Dick Flood. The galleries in Kalispell and Bigfork opened after we did. The Murphys were instigators of one of our first advertised art shows. We showed some paintings, which didn't sell, but Dick had devised a platform on which to place a piece of paper that revolved slowly while people put drips of paint on it. This created a abstract effect with various colors and different size drips. We sold these creations for one dollar each to people purchasing their own work.

With one art show a year, we did not sell a single painting the first three years. The fourth year we showed a lady artist named Althea Henry. We sold three of her paintings. The next year we showed Sheryl Bodily and sold over twenty paintings. We had one more show in our own gallery and then began renting the pool room of the Yellowstone Motor Inn and showing 10 artists each year. By this time Western art was very popular, and most of the better artists could not get enough art ahead for a one-man show so, by showing ten artists at a show, we could have a good number of paintings with from ten to a dozen from each painter. The shows were very successful. We literally had people come from as far as Denver and California. If the artists had any paintings left after the show, we generally bought them. We could not get art on consignment but had to purchase it for showing and sale in the Gallery. This fun didn't last forever. Soon there were galleries everywhere with art shows in some nearly every week.

We also participated in large art shows in Great Falls, Montana; Spokane and Seattle, Washington; and Sun Valley, Idaho. We would rent dealer rooms and generally consign to an auction in conjunction with the show. These shows were very well attended, giving us the opportunity to meet buyers from all over the country. They, in turn, would visit our gallery when near Livingston. Vi and I met many people through these contacts and still are visited by some and still visit them when traveling. A bonus to this part of our business was the opportunity to collect paintings and sculpture we liked for ourselves. For quite a few years, we gave each of our kids a painting for Christmas, which made them collectors, almost to a fault, as they were purchasing art instead of necessities.

Changes

After 25 years, we sold the portrait portion of our business to Scott Black. Scott was a young acquaintance with an interest in photography and starting a business. I sold him on the idea of working with me until he felt secure and then purchasing all of the portrait and dark room equipment. By that time we had discontinued amateur black and white processing, only processing our own color and

*Here's Fred getting his photo taken with a Brahma bull
that was part of a specialty act at the Livingston Roundup in the late 1960s.*

black and white portraits. This worked out well for Scott, who later
left photography for the restaurant business. With less work in the
store, we purchased Western Photo Sales from Don Cowles. This
was a wholesale film operation with customers in Glacier Park, Yellowstone Park Company, and many gift shops and stores as far as
West Yellowstone and Jackson Hole. This was a fun business in as

much as there were large gross sales with very small mark up. We handled lots of money, hoping a little would rub off.

After 30 years, a man approached me to purchase the business. He didn't work out, but it put the bug in my ear. In the next year Jim Blatter—a Montanan from Havre, transplanted to Seattle—wanted to return to the Big Sky. In 1986, we struck a deal, and with my usual ability to make my smartest moves by pure accident, Jim turned out to be a excellent choice for a purchaser. A handshake with Jim Blatter is better than a ten-page contract. I carried the paper, and Jim never missed a payment.

The people of Livingston and Park County were awfully good to me. Taking pictures in the schools, senior pictures, and wedding pictures put me in contact with nearly everyone at some time or another. To this day, when I see an attractive lady, I have the distinct feeling I have photographed her. The other day I asked a visitor at church if I'd done her senior pictures. "Not unless you lived in Denver, Colorado," she informed me. I always enjoyed going to work, being one of the few businesses that opened at 8 a.m. or before, but after turning the key over to Jim Blatter, I never missed it.

CHAPTER TWELVE

RECREATION

I will lift up mine eyes unto the hills, from whence cometh my help.
My help cometh from the Lord, which made heaven and earth.

Psalms 121:1-2

In this modern day, we have recreation vehicles, and we have recreation with professional sports. People recreate with TV and movies or by watching a nasal-voiced guy or gal gyrate around a stage. Many of what we call service jobs revolve around providing recreation or helping people be entertained.

For me, since as far back as I can remember, recreation meant the mountains or the river. This recreation comes in myriad forms—skiing, swimming, fishing, hiking, or trail riding. But in whatever form one indulges, a mountain or a body of water is a prerequisite.

After work on a hot summer day, Vi would take the kids and me to Ninth Street bridge. We would float on inner tubes to Mayor's Landing. What a grand trip before supper! My mother began inner tube floating in her sixties. We, perhaps foolishly, floated our kids even before they could swim. They wore a life jacket and, draped over an inner tube, bumped over the rocks and rapids. This is just one of the river's many entertainments. Bill Strong and I water skied on the river. The thrill was not the skiing but turning the boat at high speed in the narrow channel. Bill had a very inventive nature when it came to new and exciting ways to utilize the river.

One year, just prior to high water, Bill ran a cable to an island across the channel; it was tied to a tree on each side and was about twelve feet above the water. When the water was up and the current was rapid, he looped a rope over the cable from each end of his boat. By lengthening the rear rope, the current would propel the boat across the river. Then by shortening the rear rope, it would reverse and come back to the original side. Bill and Mary were having a large Fourth of July picnic and many people and scads of kids. Bill and I made a couple of trial runs. Shorten or lengthen a rope, tie it off, and scoot across the channel. Then we took a guy across that wanted to fish the island. Good run. By this time, kids were jumping up and down for a ride. We were preparing for the first load when Howard Strong, Bill's dad, really blew his stack. "You dang fools can horse around all you want to, but you're not going to drown one of these kids if I can help it." This kind of dampened the party, but Bill soon recovered. He decided we should cross over to check on the fisherman. He pulled up the front rope, making the longer rope on the rear but didn't tie it off. I told him to tie if off.

"I can hold it," from Bill.

"Tie that sucker off. You can't hold it in this current."

"I can hold it. Shove off."

I shoved off, and we started across. About half way, the rope slipped out of his hands and snapped when it hit the end. This turned the boat over, and the rear rope also broke loose from the cable. We came up with an upside down boat beside us. About twenty feet ahead, I had a brand new pair of cowboy boots floating in the current, along with two life jackets. Being safety-minded but foolish, we had life jackets but failed to have them on. We decided to swim the boat to shore. It was upside down, but floatation devises kept it from sinking. We swam and pushed, but about a mile downstream, we still seemed to be in the middle of the river. We had clothes on and were getting tired.

Bill said, "A man could drown in this river. Let's let the boat go and get out of here." We swam to shore. People had been following on shore and in cars keeping track of us. We got a ride back to the picnic, but still had a large problem... the fisherman on the island.

We called the sheriff's office, getting Sheriff Albert Nickleson, who came out with a small boat and outboard. First he brought the man back from the island; fortunately, he wasn't over the limit on fish. Then he headed downstream looking for the boat. He found the boat hung up somewhere past Mayor's Landing and even found one of the life jackets on the way, but he didn't find my new boots.

But the river isn't the only form of recreation. The mountains provide numerous ways of enjoyment—hiking, camping, backpacking, and in later years motorcycling. Many of us kids had gone to the top of Mt. Baldy during junior high school. With boy scouts and many times individually, we hiked for overnight fishing trips to Pine Creek Lake and sometimes over the top to the lakes on the other side. Bill and his dad and I made one trip to Pine Creek Lake with the idea of sleeping over. It started raining and would not quit. We were trying to stay dry under an overhanging rock. Bill's dad started reciting poetry. It was the Robert Service variety and went on and on. I asked him how he could remember all that stuff. Howard said, "If it doesn't amount to anything, I can remember it." Another time, when we were working our way down a mountain in down timber, Howard made the astute observation, "I doubt if the hand of man has ever set foot in this place."

Many people do not care for engine noise, Bill Strong being one of these, so when motorcycle trail riding came into vogue, he deserted me. My brother-in-law, Wes Strong, and his brother Dennis filled in. Talk about exhilarating times, going over the south fork of Deep Creek and back in an afternoon! We did Ramshorn Lake up Tom Miner basin and various trails in the Crazies. Once we went in above Jardine, over the top to Charlie White Lake, then up the trail to Thompson Lake, and came out in the Mill Creek drainage. My son Tom and his buddies also rode when not in school.

MOUNT HIGH

There used to be a race about fifteen miles out of Harlowton, Montana, called the Mount High at Two Dot Cross Country Race. This course was about fifteen miles long with the race being twice around. Tom and I decided we should enter this event, not with the idea of winning but just to do the course. We only rode what were known as trial bikes—250 cc engines, low torque with climbing ability but very little speed. The real racers rode up to 500 cc trail bikes that had a higher clearance along with speed as well as low torque. Our first problem was that Tom's pickup conked out in Harlowton. We found a gas station that would fix it but had to ride our trail bikes fifteen miles to get to the race starting place.

These trail bikes only went about 25 miles per hour at top speed. There were several hundred entrants in the race, and they were started off in groups of five. Just a hundred yards or so from the start, there was a creek to cross. It was only two feet deep, but those crazy riders would hit it so hard it would water out their carburetors. When I got to the creek crossing, one motorcycle was floating downstream, half submerged and bumping along on the bottom. There must have been twenty or more guys working at blowing the water out of fuel lines and carburetors. As I eased through the creek, the thought actually occurred to me that, maybe, I could win.

Right after the crossing, it was back to the creek, and the course went right upstream in the middle of said creek. It was rocky and rough with rocks and then out of the creek and up a steep hill with lots of down timber. Bikers began going around me like I was standing still. Some of those bikes seemed to only hit the ground about every fifteen or twenty feet. It reminded me of skiers coming down hill and only hitting the snow occasionally, but this was up hill. About ten miles through the course, on some switchbacks, I was taking a break, viewing the countryside. A biker came up behind me and paused. It was Kevin Albrecht, a Livingston racer. He wanted around me even when I told him there were lots of bikes ahead of him. Kevin said, "Yeah, I know, but this is my second round."

Tom and I both finished one round and then had the next surprise. Most of these bikers had wet wash cloths and towels and were cleaning themselves up with a clean change of clothes. We were mud from head to foot with nothing but the creek to freshen up in. Then it was back to Harlow for the pickup, until some good

Fred on a pack trip about 1965.

guy squeezed our bikes on his truck and gave us a ride. Even a loser is a winner after a great ride like that.

PACKING IN

Packing in with horses is in a class by itself, however, and gives camping a dimension of Western flavor and cowboying that carrying food and bed on your own back lacks. My first pack trip was with Lawrence Laugeness and Bill and Wes Strong. We were somewhere in the fourteen to sixteen year old age. We were real amateurs with the diamond hitch on our pack horses having a different configuration each day. We went over Wallace Pass out of Mill Creek with four or five different camps in the Hell Roaring drainage, including Carpenter, Charlie White, and Thompson lakes. Horses have a characteristic of wanting to go home, and ours certainly were not exceptions. We had horse trouble every night, losing at least part of them and having to use those still in camp to run the deserters down. The first morning we had two horses left, the rest were either dragging a log, hopping along with hobbles, or trailing a halter or stake-out rope. We all agreed we would never go back home to face the music if we lost those horses. Just what the alternative would have been, I don't remember. We soon discovered the direction the horses took was always toward home and in a mile or two would have the whole string back. Also part of the problem, we felt, was a bear or moose coming through camp during the night, spooking them.

Our last night out was somewhere on upper Mill Creek. We packed up in the morning, but one is always in a bigger rush heading home, so when we reached Wily Hayes place, which is now called the Bow and Arrow, we left all our pack gear with him. With empty pack horses, the pace picked up considerably, and we reached Mill Creek bridge over the Yellowstone about noon. We pooled our resources, which came to the grand total of $1.15, one dollar of which belonged to our money man, Laugeness. We stopped at a farm on the west end of the bridge and offered the lady of the house $1.15 for a little lunch. She said, "You bet," and fed us a great meal with apple pie for dessert.

MULES

Horses are interesting animals, but mules are even more so. Bill Strong and I borrowed a couple mules from Allan Nelson. We packed them both and went over the south fork of Deep Creek into the Davis Creek drainage. We set up a nice camp, hobbling and staking the animals. During supper, we looked up to see that one of the mules, with front legs hobbled, was just about at the top of the switch backs heading back down Deep Creek. We decided to let him go. A couple days later, when we came out, he was peacefully feeding in the ranger station pasture. Being hobbled for two days and traveling about eight miles hadn't even sored him. Mules are smarter than horses and do not hurt themselves.

On another trip to the lake plateau country out of the Main

Boulder, Doc Harris rented a young mule to pack. On this trip, we never moved camp but rode to various places, always returning to the same camp. We could leave the other horses, but that mule kicked up such a fuss the first day that we rode back and got him. We led him for awhile and then turned him loose. He would take the lead for awhile, and if we changed direction, he would run back and follow for awhile. We passed one camp where a dog came out barking. That mule laid his ears back, chasing the dog back off the trail. One day he was ahead of us on the trail and met two women hiking. When we caught up, the women were oohing and ahhing over him, with the mule quite obviously enjoying every minute of it. The youngest lady said, "This is the cutest horse I've ever seen," as she stroked his long ears.

On the way out, our truck and other transportation were at the Bennet Creek Ranger Station. We were running late, getting the animals loaded just about dark. On reaching Big Timber, we ate and headed for Livingston on Interstate 90. Three or four miles out of town, the truck quit us, with just enough speed to pull out of the traffic lanes. Doc and I with a pickup and horse trailer headed back to Big Timber, leaving his son Greg with the truck. When we came back with a wrecker, Greg was inside the stock rack calming the mule. The truck and car traffic rushing by made him nervous; just being with horses wasn't enough, our mule craved human reassurance.

Just one more mule story... Bill Koch tells of being at the trailhead of Big Creek, helping Jed Smith pack in a hunting camp. Jed was a local outfitter when out-of-state hunters were beginning to be big business. A kid from Missouri had drifted into Livingston, needing a job, and Jed had put him on to help the cook. The kid carried a tin suitcase and asked Jed where to put it. "Put it on that mule over there and speak to him when you walk up on him."

"I ain't never talked to no mule, and I ain't gonna start now." Walking toward the back end of that mule, he was holding the suitcase in front of him and lifting it up when that mule let him have it with both hind feet. There were two mule shoe imprints on that tin suitcase, and the kid went sprawling. Picking himself up, he said, "What did you say that mule's name was?"

This just scratches the surface of the exciting recreation Park County offers. As our kids grew, the activities changed from tent camping and short hikes to water skiing and mountain climbing. Winter also held its charms with cross-country and downhill skiing and later snowmobiling. I consider the snow machine as an old man's skis.

ANOTHER TYPE OF RECREATION

I'm not sure these little forays would qualify as recreation, but after selling the business and semi-retiring, other types of endeavors became more appealing. Having always had an interest in politics and the workings of public entities, I decided to run for the school board. After meeting with various groups, including teachers and administrators, and running a news ad or two, I was soundly defeated. But this only whetted my appetite, and I became more ambitious.

Next, I ran for the Montana House of Representatives. I didn't raise but a few dollars from close friends and did the rest of the campaign financing myself, so the financial out-go was minimal. I lost again.

Two years later, I again ran for the House. Again, my expenses were minimal, but I knocked on every door in Livingston. Of course, about a third to a half of the people were not home. This was truly a fun thing to do! I did find that all folks did not agree with my approach to state government and that, not being reticent about my opinions, might have alienated a few of the electorate. I lost again.

This should have convinced a normal person that being elected into a job may not be the best approach to getting the position. However, after a few years, I decided to try again. This time I tried for public administrator. This job involves reviewing and disposing of estates that left no will listing how to dispose of assets. Wow, I did it again… Very few people can bat 1,000 on any endeavor, even in the negative, but I managed it with very little outside help.

Downtown Livingston with Mount Baldy in the background.

*The south end of Main Street. The old McLeod Island is
now home to Park High School and the middle school.*

CHAPTER THIRTEEN

CHARACTERS IN PARADISE

Most all of us have people that influenced our thinking and actions—some for the good, and some for
the bad. It's been my good fortune to have met many
of the good influences. One of the unique features of my life is
that Bill and Wes Strong and I started playing together before we
started school, and we are still playing together. In addition, our
families were close, visiting back and forth and attending the same
church. While I was growing up, Friday evening was set aside for
visiting. This meant that ether a family would come to our house
or we would visit someone's home. These were fun times, especially if there were kids. We would rough house, and the parents
would visit and play cards.

It was after the war, however, that noticing and appreciating
people older than myself became important. I recall a fellow my
age saying what he really liked about the American Legion was

going to meetings and listening to the old heads from World War One. It wasn't just the Legion's old heads, however, that had lead interesting lives. For example, one of the Harvat brothers who ran six or eight bands of sheep in Park County had played football with Notre Dame—now, that was big time for a Park County person! Even more interesting was the pure Montana history… Donald Strong driving stagecoach in Yellowstone Park; or my dad running Holt Caterpillar tractors in eastern Montana, breaking sod with five 20-inch bottom plows; or even in my day mowing hay with horse teams, with the lore of old teamsters, roaching the manes of their matched teams, and with harness rich with brass studs and ivory rings on the spreader reins. These are little things of a bygone age that did not affect the rise and fall of empires, but did contribute to the development of our state and definitely the temper of our county.

Harvats

My first acquaintance with the Harvats was when they gave my mother bum lambs. These were lambs the ewe didn't have enough milk for, so we bottle fed them cow's milk. The Harvats were the largest ranchers in the county, owning most of the land on the Wineglass from the Park Road to Cokedale, all of Harvats' flat across the river, and many sections in other parts of the county in addition to leased forest land. Many a band of sheep came from the home ranch east of town, across Harvat's bridge (now Mayor's

Landing), across the H Street bridge, then west on Park Street and continuing on Highway 89 south to pasture up Rock Creek, Hell Roaring drainage, and other areas.

Many men were employed by the Harvats over the years for lambing, herding, and shearing. One of their longest time employees was Johnny Hankins. His main job was camp tender. This entails packing in supplies to herders in remote areas. I heard one man say John had probably slept on the ground more than any man in Park County. This is a rather dubious distinction but probably correct. Sometimes John Haberstroh would accompany Hankins on these trips, photographing pack strings, bands of sheep, and the landscape in general. Mr. Haberstroh worked and marketed his photographs through Sax and Fryer. On one of these trips, Haberstroh was smoothing out a place for his bed, using a spoon to dig out little rocks. Hankins rolled out his bed after supper and crawled in. Haberstroh asked, "Don't you even kick the big rocks out of the way to put your bed down?"

Hankins' answer was, "If the good Lord hadn't meant them rocks to be there, he wouldn't have put them there." John Hankins took horse pack strings over Wallace Pass into Hell Roaring before the trail was built. It is a tough trip with a trail; it seems impossible to this observer without one.

DAN MILES

Dan Miles, another colorful local, owned and managed his father

A.W. Miles enterprises along with his sisters. There was no pretense in Dan and very little appearance of a business man. He did wear a tie, but as an acquaintance observed one morning, "I can tell what you had for breakfast this morning by just looking at your tie, Dan." Dan's car was old, low in one corner due to a broken spring leaf, with all the fenders indicating past encounters. In the winter, Dan would cover the hood of his car with a couple of Navajo rugs. My wife told him they were valuable and that someone might possibly cart them off when he left them by the sidewalk during the day. This impressed Dan, so he put them in the house. Dogs had been lifting their leg on them outdoors for so long that Elsie, his wife, couldn't stand them. After a dry cleaning, those rugs regained their rightful place on the floor.

Dan's interests were vast—from running a band of sheep on his ranch to groceries and dry goods to hardware, lumber, and coal. And he had numerous hobbies—observing nature's many facets and even digging for fossils and minerals. One day, after spending some time on the ranch with probably some corral residue on his boots, he began inspecting a lingerie display set up in his store by a traveling salesman. "Get out of there, and leave that stuff alone," the salesman said. "Well, you just better pack up and get out of here yourself. I run this store," replied Dan.

Dan had many theories and insights. He could tell when high water was finished by the size of a patch of snow on Mt. Baldy. He once told me, "You'll see the day when Yellowstone Park will be closed to all cars with no overnight accommodations, and buses will be the only form of transportation." He must have been reading the minds of some modern-day advocates of limiting the Park's use. He told me that Harvat's flat across the river would be covered with houses. This has not happened, but it was proposed not too long ago to build a bridge across the river at the end of Main Street past the high school. He also once told me, "If I gave you the Park Hotel block, you'd have trouble making any money on it." I should have said, "Try me, Dan."

DENNIS STRONG

Those great old guys, who have all passed on now, certainly made an impression on me, but the guy whose quips and quotes impressed me most was Dennis Strong. He had the audacity to play hooky from school in the third grade. He skipped a day from West Side School with now retired Judge Byron Robb. There were rumors at West Side School that the ultimate punishment, reserved for only the greatest malfeasance, was a rubber hose administered to the proper area. In later years, I asked Den if this was true. He told me, "You'll never know." Dennis just didn't like school and quit for good somewhere in junior high. He went into the army during the Korean War, got his high school equivalence with no trouble, and learned to survey along with combat duties. Surveying has always struck me as requiring a lot of savvy, especially in rugged terrain. Dennis would survey stone quarries for his and his brother Wes Strong's travertine business.

This business used heavy equipment, and sometimes someone

would have to haul a Caterpillar to Billings for repair. They became tired of this expensive method of repair so Den tore into a diesel engine. I told him, "You don't know anything about a diesel. You've never been to diesel school."

Den's reply was, "If an idiot can build it, an idiot can fix it."

Now there is a statement you could almost build a philosophical treatise around. Dennis has a stubborn streak, and although he does not quite get obnoxious about it, he cannot abide absolute authority. When his brother Wes entered the service for World War Two, he was magnanimous with his younger brother. "While I am gone, you can use any of my stuff… except my spurs and my ski jacket."

The next morning Dennis strapped on the spurs and donned the ski jacket. He went to the corral where there were puddles of water from a night's rain. He threw a saddle on old Bonnie horse, tightened up the cinch, and stepped on. He must have hooked her with a spur climbing on as she exploded. On the first jump, Wes' ski jacket hooked over the saddle horn. Dennis said, "I couldn't fall off. With every jump, I'd leave the saddle about two feet, but the elastic in that jacket would pop me right back on." Bonnie soon settled down. Den was covered with mud, one spur was up around his thigh, the other had fallen off, and the ski jacket was a disaster. That was Dennis' contribution to his brother's war effort for that day.

Dennis enjoyed escaping from the everyday mold. If someone had a stalled car to retrieve or needed help skidding an elk, Den was always available. We were hunting elk one time, along with Wes and my stepdad, Henry Hager. It was in an area we weren't familiar with, in the mountains between Butte and Boulder. We were split up, and in the afternoon, I started tracking four or five elk. I noticed there was a man track following them also. In a short time, I came to where the man had shot an elk in very dense timber. It was all dressed out, so I picked up the track of the remaining elk, but soon found the man track again. I came upon another dressed out carcass, again shot in the dense timber, which can be difficult. I was near an open ridge so I gave up the hunt, moving out of the timber. There was Dennis looking for someone to help drag the elk he had downed in the timber.

It was getting late in the day when two men on horses came by. We propositioned them to pull the elk up on top of the ridge, which would give us a more or less downhill half mile to the jeep. One of the riders was reluctant, but finally said they would bring them up out of the timber. I guided my rider to the first elk shot, and the horse pulled it up to the ridge. But Dennis and his rider didn't show. My helper was getting worried, saying the horse the other guy was riding was green and could give trouble. I assured him that Dennis could handle any horse that ever lived, and still they did not come. I started backtrailing, finally meeting them with the elk. Den had trouble finding the carcass, which he never lived down. He just never became lost or disoriented, but that time there were so many tracks in the timber that he had gotten on the wrong one.

Those two horsemen did what we had asked them to, but they could have easily dragged them on down the ridge to the road. Dennis and I started out by dragging one animal at a time, but even with it mostly downhill, the foot or so of snow made it difficult. We would drag one about 100 yards and then go back for the other. At ten minutes to ten, we reached the road and saw car lights coming from down below. It was our jeep. Wes and Henry were making one more sweep and planned to come back in the morning if we didn't show. That would have been a chilly night but, as some famous guy once said, "All's well that ends well."

During our business years Wes and Dennis ran Livingston Marble and Granite and Montana Travertine. Frequently, we would have coffee together, discussing our various problems and shortcomings. The census bureau seemed to have me on their list, and each year they would send a long questionnaire regarding my business. There was a footnote stating one could be fined or imprisoned for not filling the form out. I would throw it in a box for a month or so and then get worried. Many of the questions struck me as asinine, such as, "Is your business located in a city, village, or elsewhere?" I felt that, when they addressed me in Livingston, they were better qualified than I to answer that. Dennis said, "You don't know how to fill out a form."

"Oh yeah, what's to know?"

"You just don't understand filling out a form."

"Okay, wise guy, tell me."

Den wagged his forefinger at me and said: "There is one thing the government can't make you do."

"What's that, Den?"

"They can't make you be smart. On the first question say, 'I don't unerstan de question.' On the next, ask, 'Wut dew yew mene?' And so on."

I related to not being smart readily, even inventing a few of my own stupidities. After finishing the form, I dropped it in the mail slot. The next day it came back for lack of postage. Now I was developing qualms about sending the form in, but not having another to fill out correctly, I finished the deed. I had been receiving a census request each year, but after my not smart one, I didn't get one for several years. In the meantime, my address had changed from a box number to my street address. I would get calls from customers saying mail they had addressed to me came back with, "Unknown at this address." My last census mail was addressed to the box number. I took it back to the post office, asking, "Why don't you stamp this 'Unknown at this address'?" The postal clerk didn't say a word, but he ink-stamped the envelope and threw it over his shoulder. The business census scratched me off their list.

Park County people, most of them anyway, would give you the proverbial shirt off their backs. They work harder when helping a neighbor than for themselves. What a great time and what a great place to grow up in.

East Side School and Court House, Livingston, Montana.

CHAPTER FOURTEEN

THE NORTHERN PACIFIC

The Northern Pacific had track laid to Mission Creek by December 31, 1882. They reached Livingston fifteen days later, on January 15, 1883. This indicates that the bridge over the Yellowstone east of Livingston was started a considerable time before. Warren McGee—railroader, photographer, and historian—tells me Livingston consisted of ten tents in October 1882, probably housing the engineers for the Bozeman tunnel and the Yellowstone bridge. By the end of 1883, the Park branch, the roundhouse, and the locomotive shops were started. Businesses from Benson's Landing, east of town, began their moves to the town site of Livingston, laid out by the railroad. In 1883, there were already three brick yards in the vicinity, manufacturing brick, and there were buildings being erected on Main Street.

Livingston was a division point, with crews, locomotives, and cabooses being changed on each train east or west. Livingston also furnished the extra helper power needed for the Bozeman hill. In the very early fifties, I was fortunate to work two winters in the roundhouse. My job was to help the hostler move locomotives in and out of the house, clean the fires, and fill the tender with coal and water in preparation for the crews to couple onto the trains. The head end crew consisted of an engineer, sometimes referred to as the hogger, a fireman, and sometimes a head brakeman. The caboose carried the conductor and brakeman. Prior to air brakes, brakemen would walk the top of a freight train, setting some brake on each box car to slow the train coming downhill.

The story is told of the wives of train crewmen discussing the importance of their husbands in the railroad's operation. The engineer's wife said her husband was most important as he ran the locomotive. The fireman's wife argued that her husband was even more important because, without his keeping a fire with a good head of steam, the locomotive wouldn't operate. The brakeman's wife countered that, unless her husband set the brakes on steep hills, the whole train could be wrecked. The conductor's wife, an Irish lady, said, "When mah husban raises his han, the whole traane moves."

The locomotive shops did major repairs and were always full of engines in various stages of disarray or reassembly. The roundhouse was more of storage facility, doing minor repairs to prepare the engine for another trip. The stalls were, of course, in a circle with a turntable in the middle. When coming out of the house, engines could be turned to head either east or west, depending on what train it was ordered for. Occasionally a locomotive would go through the outside of the house. This could be while it was unattended and not properly blocked, but also with some classes of these steam engines, the brakes were slow to set up, causing the engineer or hostler to use the Johnson bar, the device they used to change directions, to stop it. One hostler moved into the house a little too fast, and he pulled the Johnson bar into reverse so hard that he came backing onto the turntable again. When he started back into the house, he yelled at his helper, "When I get it in this time, slam the door shut on it."

For various infractions of rules, most of them pertaining to safety, a crewman could be put on suspension, pending an official hearing. On one such occasion, a local crew was setting out cars at the cement plant in Trident between Livingston and Helena. The yardmaster at Trident was very particular on how cars were spotted, giving the brakeman a lot of guff. The brakie, getting a little upset, referred to the yardmaster as an SOB. This in turn upset the yardmaster, who registered a complaint, causing the brakeman to go on suspension. When the hearing was held, an official asked the brakeman, "Did your call Mr. So-and-So an SOB?" He replied: "Yes, I did."

"Why would you do that?" He came back with: "I thought it was his name as everybody called him that."

Working in the roundhouse, one could see all the characters depicted in the J.R. Williams' cartoons—the tall, the short, and the small. Some liked to work while some did as little as possible. There was always a certain amount of tomfoolery going on with some contributing more than their fair share. Homer Langley, father of Homer Langley, Park County assessor for many years, was one of these. Homer worked when there was work to do; the rest of the time he played cards or jokes on fellow workers. The more frequent recipients of the jokes were those who reacted most dramatically. One who had suffered from Homer's hobby was seeking vengeance. He crept up behind Homer with a large firecracker. Homer was dealing a hand of pitch at a work table. When the small bomb went off, everyone jumped except Homer. Without a break in his dealing or even turning his head, Homer said, "Joe, if you have to fart, go outside."

The railroad was Livingston's principal industry for many years, and it is still a large employer. Many young men worked a summer or two while going to college, and many made it their life's work, making a good living to raise a family and own a home. Although some thought the railroad had many shortcomings, it actually provided a stable life for many people and a rich heritage for all of Livingston and Park County.

CHAPTER FIFTEEN

MAY I EDITORIALIZE?

Many writers have extolled Montana. It was and still is known as the Treasure State, but you rarely hear of "the land of shining mountains." A.B. Guthrie's book, "The Big Sky," provided a new name for our state, and Ivan Doig enlarged on this idea with his first book, "This House of Sky." This preoccupation with sky must imply that our sky is different, or perhaps it's because we have more sky than some states, due to size. More recently, Kittredge and Smith edited a Montana anthology, dubbing our state in their book, "The Last Best Place." These are all very pleasing and nice-sounding appellations, appealing to anyone's senses. There is, however, another side to this pleasing coin, with a large group of people saying that we have not handled our resources properly and that we are destroying our habitat, denuding our forests, and polluting our streams. I respectfully submit that, if Montana has been destroying herself, how can we be "The Last Best Place"?

I cannot speak for the entire state, but Park County has been logging for more than 100 years and still has more timber than it had when it started. One has only to look at old photographs to see that timber has moved down the mountains and filled in many areas that were devoid of trees years ago. Game numbers may not have increased, but it is certainly easier to bag a deer now than it was in the thirties. Elk also were in few areas with a large percentage of the hunting in the Gardiner-Jardine area when Yellowstone Park elk migrated out during deep snow. Now elk have spread into nearly all mountainous areas of Montana, and they particularly like clear cut logging areas for the grass it provides.

There have been some mining and timbering indiscretions in the past, mostly done in ignorance, and these practices have been called to public attention by environmental groups and, over time, were corrected, for everyone's best interest. However, there are now groups that persist in challenging every timber sale, including blow down and fire damaged trees in every area. There are groups that feel hunting is detrimental, that cattle raising destroys the land, that flood control projects are against nature, and even that power-producing dams should be removed. There are some groups that appear to be against people and propose that buffalo should be returned to the plains.

In the first chapter of Genesis, God gave man dominion over every living thing, and man was told to subdue the earth. My dictionary defines "subdue" as "to bring into subjection, conquer, vanquish and in a somewhat kinder tone, to control." Similarly, "dominion" is "to rule or power to rule." Can anyone quote a higher authority or go further back in history to establish that the world was made for man, not the other way around?

With millions of acres of wilderness for quiet and solitude, there are those that would deny the use of the rest for motorized recreation. I was brought up in the engine age and feel that three of the sweetest sounds in the world are a John Deere B, a Harley 74, and four 1200-horse Pratt and Whitney's winding up for takeoff with a heavy load and a short runway. We are in a modern world, and we must realize that even man is part of the so-called ecosystem.

I am not devoid of environmental concerns, however, being particularly anxious about the breaking up of our agricultural land. Being a great believer in life, liberty, and pursuit of happiness, I feel anyone should be able to live where they want, but does everyone need 20 to a 100 acres just to build a house? Especially when the acreage is prime farm land? In national rankings that various groups are compiling, Montana generally ranks on the bottom or, occasionally with a little luck, second from the bottom. If and when a study is ever made on 20-acre home sites per capita, I'll bet on Montana being in the top 1%.

Excuse me, folks, but a man has to bellyache once in a while.

Good things have followed me all the days of my life: a happy childhood, a loving wife, good kids, and great grandkids. I have done everything I ever wanted to do with the possible exception of spending one season on an Alaskan fishing boat and operating a grain combine from Oklahoma to Canada, but there isn't time for everything. I have been richly blessed, and people have always been nice to me. I could check out of this beautiful world anytime with a phrase from modern vernacular: "I've been there, I've done that."